CW01249473

Vindiciæ Veritatis

OR A

CONFUTATION

OF THE
HERESIES AND GROSS ERROURS
ASSERTED BY

THOMAS COLLIER

IN HIS

ADDITIONAL WORD

TO HIS

BODY OF DIVINITY.

Written by *Nehemiah Coxe*, a Servant of Jesus Christ, and Minister of his Gospel.

For there must be also Heresies among you, that those which are approved may be made manifest among you, 1 Cor. 11. 19.

Ye therefore beloved, seeing ye know these things before, beware lest ye also, being led away with the errour of the wicked, fall from your own steadfastness, 2 Pet. 3. 17.

Πανοῦργοί εἰσι καὶ ἐπιθέται οἱ αἱρετικοὶ, διὰ τοῦτο λέγει, Προσέχετε. Χρηστολογίαν μὲν γὰρ προβάλλονται, καὶ βίον ὑποκρίνονται σεμνὸν, ἀλλ᾽ ἔσωθέν ἐστι τὸ ἄγκιστρον. *Theoph.*

Nonnulli dum plus exquirunt contemplando, quam capiunt, usque ad perversa dogmata erumpunt: et dum veritatis discipuli esse negligunt humiliter, magistri erroris fiunt. *Greg.*

LONDON,

Printed for *Nath. Ponder*, at the *Peacock* in the *Poultry* near *Corn-hill*, and in *Chancery-lane* near *Fleet-street*, 1677.

The First quotation on the title page is from the eleventh-century Bishop Theophylact of Ohrid's commentary on Matthew's Gospel, *ΕΡΜΗΝΕΙΑ ΕΙΣ ΤΟ ΚΑΤΑ ΜΑΤΘΑΙΟΝ ΕΥΑΓΓΕΛΙΟΝ* (*Enarratio in Evangelium Matthæi*) which may be found in J.P. Migne's *Patrologiæ Cursus Completus* (Paris: 1849), *Patrologiæ Græcæ Tomus* CXXIII:213. It is a gloss on Matthew 7.15-16, which reads *"Beware of false prophets, which come to you in sheep's clothing, but inwardly they are ravening wolves. Ye shall know them by their fruits. Do men gather grapes of thorns, or figs of thistles?"* Theophylact's comment may be translated "The heretics are knaves and plotters. For this reason, He says, 'Beware!' For indeed they push forth convincing speech, and they pretend a pious life, but the snare is within."

The second quotation on the title page is from Gregory the Great's *Moralia in Job* Liber Sextus, Caput XXXVII [Vet. XXVI.] 57 (http://www.mirabileweb.it/title/moralia-in-iob-gregorius-i-papa-n-540-ca-m-604/4255). It does not exactly match the version in Migne's *Patrologiæ* LXXIX:1191, but more closely resembles that in Thomas Aquinas, *Summa Theologica*, II-II Q. 188, Article 5 (https://aquinas.cc/la/en/~ST.II-II.Q188.A5). It has been translated as "some through seeking in contemplation more than they are able to grasp, fall away into perverse doctrines, and by failing to be the humble disciples of truth become masters of error." St. Thomas Aquinas, *Summa Theologica* (Notre Dame, IN: Christian Classics, 1948), IV:1991.

This book has been edited by James M. Renihan

Publication Information:

Copyright, Broken Wharfe, 2023
ISBN: 978-1-7399727-7-6

Printed by TJ Books Limited

PUBLISHER'S NOTE

This treatise is a supreme example of the theological precision and application shared among the early confessors of the Second London Baptist Confession of Faith. Written by Nehemiah Coxe and endorsed by leading confessional Baptist ministers, this book exemplifies the practice of confessional Baptist associational life. Calling upon and supporting young Coxe to engage with several "heresies and gross errors" brought about by Thomas Collier, the churches publicly refuted and declared their faith in the face of theological confusion. We hope these minor amendments help readers observe Coxe's labour in "rightly dividing the word of truth" as he contended for "the faith which was once for all delivered to the saints".

It is a privilege to provide the reader with this historical republication. We took great care to reflect the original manuscript whilst making it easier for the modern reader to digest. Very few minor amendments have been made in formatting. Like many documents of the period, there are few, if any, spaces between the lines of the original. In this edition, spacing is added between paragraphs, and a minor change in formatting is made where there are subpoints in an argument or lengthy quotes from other authors.

Moreover, there are a few places where lists have been set apart and spaced, which the original manuscript left as part of a paragraph. The reader will also note that when Coxe cites and summarises Thomas Collier, consideration is given. In order to aid the reader in identifying Collier's ideas, the italics are preserved. However, Coxe provides other words and phrases in italics when he is not citing Collier. These are very few. Let the reader discern. Additionally, we have taken the liberty to format in **bold typeface** where Scripture is cited as indicated in the original manuscript by inverted commas, otherwise known as quotation marks.

Apart from these minor adjustments in formatting, Dr James Renihan and his team of colleagues have done a remarkable job providing this significant work, paying careful attention to the original. They have crafted a modern edition that includes a meticulous transcription of the original, notes for Hebrew words and expressions and translation of Greek terms and Latin words and phrases. Dr James Renihan has served the church of the living God well through his meticulous editing of this manuscript. Christ is worthy.

- Broken Wharfe

ENDORSEMENTS

❖

"The re-publication of Vindiciæ Veritatis is a significant event. It is more important than the various seventeenth century works on believer's baptism because it defends and asserts the fundamentals of the Christian faith. We are indebted to the editorial skills of Dr Jim Renihan and his team for this edition. Nehemiah Coxe deserves to be better known and perhaps he would be had he lived to participate in the National Assembly in 1689. In dealing with the 'manifold errors' of Thomas Collier, Coxe shows his own understanding of historic biblical Christianity and the orthodox credentials of our Particular Baptist forefathers expressed in the Second London Baptist Confession of Faith. Coxe called his readers to steadfastness in the faith. That very quality is needed in the twenty-first century and this volume will aid readers to that end."

Austin Walker, formerly a pastor of Maidenbower Baptist Church, Crawley, UK and author of The Excellent Benjamin Keach.

"This book is a powerful reminder that serious churches may need to deal with serious errors – even among their leaders. But it also reminds us of the resources for the defence of orthodoxy with which we have been provided in the history of the church. Sensitively edited and carefully presented, this new edition of Coxe's Vindiciæ Veritatis shows how seriously the earliest Particular Baptists contended for the faith once delivered to the saints."

Crawford Gribben, professor of history at Queen's University Belfast, Northern Ireland.

"When William Screven's church in Kittery Maine was recognized in 1682 by the Baptist church In Boston as competent in numbers and faith to be set aside as an independent Baptist congregation, they commended their faith in terms of their agreement with the Second London Confession. When William Screven retired around 1712 from his post as pastor of First Baptist Church in Charleston, SC, [they had moved from Kittery in 1696 to Charleston] he recommended earnestly that they "take care that the person be orthodox in the faith and of blameless life, and does own the confession put forth by our brethren in London in 1689." Screven had come from England where he functioned as a "gifted brother" in Somerset along with Thomas Collier and signed the Somerset Confession of Faith (1656) written largely by Collier. This present volume by Nehemiah Coxe is an important part of the textual, historical, and theological witness to the two-decade doctrinal dilution and corruption of Collier and the careful posturing of Screven to establish distance between himself and Collier's defection. Subsequent to the appearance of Nehemiah Coxe's astute interaction with Collier and the 1677 confessional action of London Baptists, Collier wrote another confession in 1678. These events highlight both the timing and the content of Nehemiah Coxe's clear polemical engagement with Collier under the witness of historic Christian orthodoxy and confessional Reformed doctrine. Enjoy the tightly argued and clearly expressed text of Coxe and embrace the calling to contend earnestly for the faith once delivered to the saints."

Tom J. Nettles, Senior Professor of Historical Theology, The Southern Baptist Theological Seminary, Louisville, Kentucky, USA

In the mid 1670s the English Particular Baptists faced a major crisis. One of their most popular and successful evangelists Thomas Collier challenged the historic orthodox doctrines of the person and work of Christ. It was to counteract Collier's heterodox influence that Nehemiah Coxe, a London pastor, wrote Vindiciæ Veritatis or Vindication of the Truth. It was a delicate situation as Coxe was a young pastor challenging a man who was well-known and heretofore deeply respected. The Latin title and the frequent appeal to Greek and Latin authors, - all helpfully translated in this edition - would suggest that Coxe was reaching out to an erudite readership beyond his denomination and perhaps beyond England. It was such a sensitive issue for Particular Baptists who had always insisted that they had no connections with the heterodox Continental Anabaptists. Coxe's work was timely. The political world was convulsed by the Exclusion Crisis which produced a reaction which reignited hostility and suffering for Nonconformists when in the words of Gerald Cragg 'a wild irresponsibility had infused itself into English public life'. Nehemiah Coxe's work is however not just a fascinating insight into a historical crisis, it is an able defence of teachings that are always the subject of Satanic attack and as such remains highly relevant.

Robert W. Oliver, formerly pastor of the Old Baptist Chapel, Bradford On Avon, Wiltshire, UK, Church History teacher and author of History of the English Calvinistic Baptists, 1771-1892.

"In the theological battles of the seventeenth century, a young but gifted Baptist divine named Nehemiah Coxe penned a defense of the doctrines of God, the Trinity, election, particular redemption, original sin, perseverance, justification, and eternal punishment. Coxe's book illustrates the doctrinal commitments, not only of those subscribing to the Second London Baptist Confession, but also of Reformed churches in general, as Coxe's citations of William Ames, John Owen, and Gisbertus Voetius demonstrate. May God be pleased to use this work again to strengthen those who raise the banner of Christian orthodoxy."

Dr Joel R. Beeke, President, Puritan Reformed Theological Seminary, Grand Rapids, Michigan, USA.

Ironically, heresies have often been profitable to the cause of truth throughout the history of the church. Thomas Collier's doctrinal errors were an opportunity for the Particular Baptists, through the pen of the brilliant and young pastor Nehemiah Coxe, to publicly affirm their orthodoxy with greater clarity and to demonstrate their commitment to the historic teaching of the church.

The republication of Vindiciæ Veritatis will benefit Reformed Baptists today in at least two ways. First, by providing a theological context directly associated with the Second London Baptist Confession of Faith. Holders of that confession will be able to appreciate the meticulous articulation of key doctrines that they confess. Second, the initial controversy that gave rise to this book shows us how the congregational ecclesiology, to which the Particular Baptists were committed, would have to deal with the emergence of heresy in a particular church with which other congregations hold communion. This work, and the process that preceded it, is in some sense the exercise of the power of the keys.

Pascal Denault, pastor of Église réformée baptiste de Saint-Jérôme and author of The Distinctiveness of Baptist Covenant Theology

Many years ago, James M. Renihan sent me a copy of Nehemiah Coxe's Vindiciæ Veritatis. I was fascinated with it then as I am now. It displays orthodox polemics, wide reading, deep thinking, careful distinctions, and tight argumentation. It addresses important issues concerning Christian orthodoxy, many of which are debated in our own day. I find Coxe's method of addressing issues fascinating and very instructive. This is not an easy read. It demands careful attention by the reader. I commend it highly as a good example of a seventeenth-century theologian seeking to vindicate the truth against heresies and gross errors.

Richard C. Barcellos, pastor of Grace Reformed Baptist Church, Palmdale, California, USA and Associate Professor of Exegetical Theology, International Reformed Baptist Seminary, Mansfield, Texas, USA

Vindiciæ Veritatis
Or a
Confutation
of the
Heresies and Gross Errours
Asserted by
Thomas Collier
in his
Additional Word
to his
Body of Divinity

Written by *Nehemiah Coxe*, a Servant of Jesus Christ, and Minister of his Gospel

For there must be also Heresies among you, that those which are approved may be made manifest among you, 1 Cor. 11.19
Ye therefore beloved, seeing ye know these things before, beware lest ye also, being led away with the errour of the wicked, fall from your own steadfastness, 2 Pet. 3.17

Πανοῦργοί εἰσι καὶ ἐπιθέται οἱ αἱρετικοί, διὰ τοῦτο λέγει, Προσέχετε. Χρηστολογίαν μὲν γὰρ προβάλλονται, καὶ βίον ὑποκρίνονται σεμνὸν, ἀλλ' ἔσωθέν ἐστι τὸ ἄγκιστρον. *Theoph.*

Nonnulli dum plus exquirunt contemplando, quam capiunt, usque ad perversa dogmata erumpunt: et dum veritatis discipuli esse negligunt humiliter, magistri erroris fiunt. *Greg.*

LONDON,
Printed for *Nath. Ponder*, at the *Peacock* in the *Poultry* near *Corn-hill*, and in *Chancery-lane* near *Fleet-street*, 1677.

CONTENTS

PUBLISHER'S NOTE iii
ENDORSEMENTS v
ACKNOWLEDGEMENTS 7
INTRODUCTION 9
CHRISTIAN READER, ... 15
TO THE READER 19
CHAPTER I 27
CHAPTER II 63
CHAPTER III 81
CHAPTER IV 113
CHAPTER V 137
CHAPTER VI 169
CHAPTER VII 179
SCRIPTURE INDEX 217

ACKNOWLEDGEMENTS

In 2005, Reformed Baptist Academic Press issued a slightly modernized version of Nehemiah Coxe's *A Discourse of the Covenants that God made with Men before the Law*.[1] This useful book provided modern readers access to material written by a leading seventeenth century Particular Baptist pastor and theologian. Now, almost twenty years later, it is a pleasure to introduce another fine work by Coxe, *Vindiciae Veritatis, Or A Confutation of the Heresies and Gross Errours asserted By Thomas Collier in his Additional Word to his Body of Divinity*. First published in 1677, it is an exceedingly valuable theological treatise, offered in repudiation of several heretical doctrinal views of a man who had been a leader among the Particular Baptist churches. Although a refutation of serious theological errors, the positive doctrinal expressions offered in Coxe's responses are of great value. They demonstrate the committed orthodoxy of the ministers of many churches and the relation that orthodoxy sustains to historic Christian dogma.

This publication is the result of the work of many people. Gatlin Bredeson transcribed the original text. Joshua D. Wilson provided notes for Hebrew words and expressions, Nick Pollock for Greek terms and many Latin words or phrases. Some Latin sentences in the

---

[1] Nehemiah Coxe and John Owen, *Covenant Theology: From Adam to Christ* (Palmdale: Reformed Baptist Academic Press, 2005).

book are difficult, and both Nick Pollock and Susan Strickland offered translations for these. Timothy Decker located and translated the quotation from Theophylact. Darrin Gilchrist of Broken Wharfe has overseen the publication process. I appreciate the collegial spirit demonstrated by all. Thank you very much.

Soli Deo Gloria.

James M. Renihan

INTRODUCTION
James M. Renihan

Nehemiah Coxe (1650-1689), son of the first-generation Particular Baptist pastor Benjamin Coxe, is an important figure in the second generation of baptized congregationalist ministers.[1] Recognized as a "gifted brother" by John Bunyan's Bedford congregation in 1671, he was called to and ordained pastor (along with William Collins) of London's Petty France church in September 1675. It has been surmised that these two men edited the document known popularly as the 1689 Confession when it was first published in 1677.

Though only about 27 years old, and having ministered in London for approximately two years, Coxe became enmeshed in a major theological dispute carried on by the pastors of several London churches and one of their own who had been sent from London to minister in his home county of Somerset in the mid-1640s. His name was Thomas Collier (1613?-1690?).[2] For three decades he had been active in the West Country planting churches and leading

---

[1] For biographical information on Benjamin Coxe see Samuel Renihan, *From Shadow to Substance* (Oxford: Centre for Baptist History and Heritage, 2018), 117-18 and for Nehemiah Coxe see Samuel Renihan, *The Petty France Church (Part 1)* (Oxford: Centre for Baptist Studies, 2019), 57-198.

[2] The most extensive study to date is Richard Land, *"Doctrinal Controversies of English Particular Baptists (1641-1691) as Illustrated by the Career and Writings of Thomas Collier"* unpublished D.Phil. thesis, University of Oxford, 1979.

associational efforts, but in the 1670s he published opinions deemed to be "heresies and gross errours." These produced great concern among members of his own congregation, other ministers in the West, and ultimately several key London pastors. He unabashedly published his views for all to see, especially in two books, *The Body of Divinity, or, A Confession of Faith* and *An Additional Word to the Body of Divinity or Confession of Faith*.[3]

Meetings and conversations between Collier and other ministers were fruitless. Collier dug in his heels, resisting every effort to call him to repentance. Because of his prominence, his long and influential ministry, and since he used the phrase "Confession of Faith" in the titles of the books deemed erroneous, the London pastors determined that a publication exposing and refuting his errors was necessary. They approached the young Nehemiah Coxe to write on their behalf; *Vindiciae Veritatis* is the product of this request.[4] It is an impressive piece of work demonstrating scholarship at a high level. Relying on the best writers from the history of the church as well as contemporary theologians, arguing from the original languages of Scripture, and expressing careful conclusions consonant with ancient Christian creeds and post-reformation confessions of faith, it contrasts Collier's deviations with orthodox doctrine as confessed by the best writers "ancient and modern."

The book commences with a letter, signed by six prominent London ministers, explaining the purpose for publication, as well as the reasons for choosing Coxe to write on their behalf. It is impressive to realize that some of these men had been part of the leadership of churches since the 1640s. They were senior men who saw wisdom in

---

[3] Thomas Collier, *The Body of Divinity, Or, a Confession of Faith* (London: Nathaniel Crouch, 1674) and Collier, *An Additional Word to the Body of Divinity, or Confession of Faith* (London: Printed for the Author, 1676).

[4] Samuel Renihan presents a cogent argument suggesting that the Second London Confession (which appeared in the midst of this controversy) was written as another response to the dangerous deviations of Collier and the possibility that the Baptized congregations would be branded with heresy by means of guilt by association. See S. Renihan, *Shadow*, 174-81.

the words of a young man.[5] This is followed by Coxe's "To the Reader," an apology (in the classical sense) for the book in hand. Coxe asserts that his own doctrine as expressed in the following pages agrees with both Scripture and "that Doctrine which the Church of God hath always been possessed of." Next, we find a summary of twenty "gross errours" contained in Collier's *Additional Word*.

The main body of the book contains seven chapters:

1. **"Concerning God; The distinct Subsistencies (*sic*) in the Divine Nature: And more especially, the Person of the Son,"** a careful presentation of trinitarianism and Chalcedonian Christology in contrast to Collier's Socinian-like tendencies;

2. **"Of Election"** in which Coxe refutes Collier's strange mixture of Pelagianism, Arminianism and assorted confusing errors;

3. **"Of the Extent of Christ's Death,"** a confutation of Collier's universalism;

4. **"Concerning the moral power of Man, or Free-will, where also of Original sin,"** a rejoinder to Collier's bewildering presentation of human nature and its sinfulness;

5. **"Wherein some things relating to the principles already asserted, are farther cleared and vindicated: And also the Saints perseverance proved, and Tho. C's exceptions removed"** an expansion of previous arguments and a treatment of the Perseverance of the Saints;

6. **"Of Justification,"** a clear exposition of a doctrine that "must needs be acknowledged to be of great importance;" and

---

[5] Collier replied to *Vindiciae Veritatis* in Thomas Collier, *A Sober and Modest Answer to Nehemiah Coxe's Invective (pretended) Refutation* (London: Francis Smith, 1677). He was not impressed, dismissing Coxe because of his youth: "and as for Mr. Coxe, he saith he is a young man, and probably, so young, that his head might scarce be warm at that time…." Collier, *Sober and Modest*, unnumbered page 2 of the Preface. The *Sober and Modest Answer* is neither sober, modest, nor an answer!

7. "**Of the Day of Judgement, and the Everlasting punishment of the wicked**," a chapter exposing Collier's advocacy of forms of universal salvation and denial of eternal punishment.

Each of these chapters probes into the relevant subjects, rebutting Collier's errors from careful exegesis of Scripture and citations from the best theologians. The list of writers quoted is impressive. It includes well-known authors such as Augustine, James Ussher, John Owen and William Ames, as well as more obscure writers, for instance, Johannes Mercer, Santes Pagninus and Frances Vatablus. Occasional epigrams and quotations from classical literature also make appearances. Clearly, the work demonstrates a high level of scholarship.

Coxe closes the book with two words of application, the first to professing believers, and the second to those who still "live in their sins." The word to "those that profess subjection to Christ" calls them to "steadfastness" in their Christian profession, that they might know the truth and live carefully in its light, both as they "confess" the faith in speech and live holy lives. To unbelievers he urges the necessity of repentance and faith, an appropriate exhortation with which to conclude a careful theological treatise.

The connection with the Second London Baptist Confession of Faith is important to note. Published in the same year (1677) and intended to be a summary of the "wholesome Protestant doctrine"[6] professed by the churches, it provides succinct summaries of the theological commitments staked out by Coxe in *Vindiciae Veritatis*. Reading the two documents side-by-side provides the student with helpful insight into the relevant chapters of the briefer Confession of Faith.

---

[6] *A Confession of Faith. Put forth by the Elders and Brethren of many Congregations of Christians (baptized upon Profession of Faith) in London and the Country (Printed in the Year, 1677)*, unnumbered page 5 of the epistle "To the Judicious and Impartial Reader." The mention of "the Country" is a hint that the Confession was published in response to the controversy with Collier.

Vindiciae Veritatis is written in the style of its own day, a form that may at times challenge twenty-first century readers. It is, however, worth the effort to understand and digest the sound doctrine it promotes. Perhaps it will be shocking to read of Thomas Collier's many "heresies and gross errours." It is right to be saddened by them and to rejoice in the truth so well-expressed in Coxe's "confutation." The encouragement brought by the careful statements of truth provided by this important Particular Baptist ought to strengthen the faith of believers today, just as it was intended to do nearly 350 years ago.

CHRISTIAN READER,

We whose names are here subscribed, thought ourselves more particularly, than many others, obliged in duty and conscience to appear in the front of this book by way of approbation of the same; wherein the manifold errors of Thomas Collier, in a book entitled [*An Additional Word*, &c.] are clearly detected, and solidly enervated: Because although it be a most unequal judgment, to make the errors of one single person under any profession, to reflect upon the whole of the same; seeing the Apostle telleth the Church in its primitive and most pure state "That there should arise from themselves men speaking perverse things, and draw away Disciples after them," (Acts 20.30) yet woeful experience hath taught us that there is nothing more usual with the world. And we did judge, that though we do not hope hereby to silence the mouth of malice; yet this might be a means, to set us right in the thoughts of those who are not biased by evil affections.

We had hoped that the snares, wherein the said Thomas Collier had been many years entangled, and for which he seemed by God's blessing on some of our endeavors, to manifest repentance, might have been a caution to him, to avoid these dangerous rocks for the future; but to our grief we find it otherwise, and see that the highest profession cannot secure men from falling, when the heart is not established with grace, and kept humble before the Lord, as we see in the examples of Hymeneus and Alexander.

For the author of this work, if any by reason of his inferiority in years, should suspect him of an over-forwardness, arising from any over-weening self-opinion, in undertaking this matter, although that answer is ready in his behalf, which sometime David gave to Eliab in a case though of a different, yet something like nature; "What have I done? Is there not a cause?" (1 Sam. 17.29) Shall the whole Host of Israel be defied, the principles of Gospel-truths subverted, the name of God blasphemed, a floodgate of error opened, and any be thought over-forward to oppose the Adversary?

But over and above we think meet to acquaint thee, that the combatant in this conflict was not so much prompted to it by his natural inclination, as by the joint and earnest persuasion of several of the Elders, and that of elder years, partly because we did judge him meet and of ability for the work, and next, at that time of his entering upon it, a more than ordinary providence of God, gave him leisure for it more than others, by suspending him from other more weighty employment; thereby (as it were) calling him out, and determining him to this employ: Wherein (upon our perusal) we hope, we may truly say, without particular respect to his person, he hath behaved himself with that modesty of spirit, joined with that fullness and clearness of answer and strength of argument, that we comfortably conceive (by God's blessing) it may prove a good and sovereign antidote against the poison: from which as we earnestly pray the venter of it may be delivered, so no less that thou also mayest be preserved; and in order thereunto, desire of thee, that thou wouldst read this ensuing discourse, with this candor and charity to believe, that it is Verity, not Victory, that is here contended for: And farther we beg of God, that thou mayest be enabled to weigh each particular in the just balance of the sanctuary; and that he will direct thy heart into the love of truth, which shall be the daily prayer of

Thine in the Lord,

William Kiffen.   *Joseph Maisters.*   *Henry Forty.*
Daniel Dyke.   *James Fitton.*   *William Collins.*[1]

---

[1] William Kiffen (1616-1701) was pastor of London's Devonshire Square church. See Larry Kreitzer, *William Kiffen and His World* (Oxford: Centre for Baptist History and Heritage, 2010 etc.), 7 volumes; Daniel Dyke (1617-1688) was ejected from Hadham Magna in Hertfordshire and later became co-pastor with Kiffen at Devonshire Square. See Samuel Palmer, *The Nonconformist's Memorial* (London: Button and Son, 1802), II:304; Joseph Maisters (1640-1714) studied under Thomas Goodwin at Magdalen College, Oxford and after adopting Baptist principles served churches in Theolbalds, Hertfordshire and Joiners Hall in London. See Thomas Crosby, *The History of the English Baptists* (London: John Robinson, 1740), III:159, IV: 342-46; James Fitton (also Fitten—?-1678?) was pastor of the Swan Alley church from 1673-78. See W.T. Whitley, *A Baptist Bibliography* (Hildesham: Georg Olms, 1984 reprint), I:217; Henry Forty (?-1692) signed the 1651 edition of the First London Confession and later served as co-pastor with Fitton of the Swan Alley church of which Henry Jessey had been pastor. See Joseph Ivimey *A History of the English Baptists* (London: Button and Son, 1814), II:66-68; William Collins (?-1702) served as co-pastor with Nehemiah Coxe at London's Petty France church. See John Piggott, *Eleven Sermons Preach'd upon Special Occasions* (London: John Darby, 1714), 241-86.

TO THE READER.

Courteous Reader,

Amongst all those vanities which are under the Sun, this is none of the least; That some men puffed up with a conceit of their sufficiency for every undertaking, do daily burden the world with their raw and indigested notions; and whilst they condemn that guidance they might have in the way of truth, from the labors of others who have been raised up and enabled of God to transmit to posterity the doctrine of the Gospel in a form of sound words, do darken counsel by words without knowledge: But alas! Our sorrow on this account may be drowned in tears for a greater evil, if we reflect on the more bold and dangerous attempts of some, who are not satisfied to have darkened the shining luster of divine truth, unless they do also subvert the foundations of the Christian religion, by a downright opposition to some of the most important doctrines thereof. And one sad instance of this kind we have in a book not long since published by Thomas Collier, which he calls *An Additional Word*, &c. which hath occasioned my writing this small treatise in answer thereto; for although the argument of the book may not seem to require this pains; inasmuch as there is nothing urged by him to give countenance to his corrupt notions, but it hath either been answered many times already by those that have written against the Pelagians, Jesuits, and Socinians, in whose steps Mr. Collier very frequently treads; or else (where he doth transcend the heresies of those mentioned) its weakness and impiety is more manifest than to need any refutation by another; yet on many accounts, some answer to him was judged necessary, not only by myself, but by divers others, whose judgment in this matter I esteemed much more than my own; that so (at least) a public testimony might be born against those gross errors therein, by him exposed to public view; and by the detection of them, the entanglement and seduction of weak (though well-meaning) souls might be prevented, who otherwise were in danger to be drawn away by him, to drink in those notions that will eat as doth a canker; and also that persons irreligious and ungodly, who are ready to catch at anything, even against the judgment of their own consciences, that may give them quiet in their sinful ways, might not rest in peace on those pillows he hath prepared for them; by his endeavor to persuade them, that there is no such eternal wrath and judgment like to overtake them, as that which they have been warned to flee from by those that know the terror of the Lord.

These with some other things of like import, prevailed with me to account it necessary, that those precious truths opposed by him, should be vindicated from his cavils and reproaches: Though for myself, I can truly say, I had much rather for many reasons, some other of my brethren had undertaken this work; and I have many witnesses this task was imposed on, not sought by me; for I have no such esteem of my ability, as to desire to trouble the world in print; and therefore I beg a candid interpretation of my appearing in public on this occasion.

In my answer I have been forced very briefly to touch upon many of Mr. Collier's notions, being desirous to bring it into as little room as might be, lest by its length it should be rendered the less serviceable to many of those for whose good it was chiefly intended; and therefore have passed over many things more remote from the main controversy, in silence, which otherwise might have deserved some remark: Amongst which you may reckon that which so often occurs in his book, viz. this and that is true in a Gospel sense, or some Scripture sense; which sense he yet gives us no account of, but what we must gather from his accommodation of that which he saith is true in a Gospel sense, to his own absurd opinions, which may serve to amuse and deceive his ignorant and unwary reader.

This I am abundantly satisfied in, that what I have asserted against Mr. Collier is plainly confirmed in the Scripture of truth, and agreeable to that doctrine which the Church of God hath always been possessed of; and are no new notions of my own coining; and therefore I hope by the grace of Christ to be enabled farther to clear and strengthen what I have written, if occasion be really offered by Mr. Collier his making such a reply as hath any color of reason urged against it; otherwise I shall not concern myself with a noise of vain words, but rest satisfied in that I have once for all born my witness against him, and detected his errors.

I earnestly desire that God would give him repentance unto the acknowledgement of the truth, that by his own recantation of what he hath published so contrary thereto, and offensive to true Christians, this contest may have an end put to it; and forasmuch as I understand Mr. Collier pretends some respect to the labors of Dr. Usher;[1] I could heartily wish, he would seriously read over his *Body of Divinity*, and his treatise of the Incarnation of the Son of God, called *Immanuel*, printed at the end thereof; that if he will not attend to what I have written, yet he may by that holy man be better informed about the principles of Christianity. And that he may for the future escape that absurdity and confusion he hath cast himself into in his first chapter concerning the Person of Christ, I desire he would

---

[1] Coxe refers to James Ussher (1581-1656), Bishop of Armagh in Ireland and Primate of the Church of Ireland. Ussher was well-regarded by English puritans. See the entry in the *Oxford Dictionary of National Biography*. James Ussher, *A Body of Divinitie* bound with *Immanuel, or, The Mystery of the Incarnation of the Son of God* (London: William Hunt, 1658).

compare this observation of the Dr. with what I have written on the same head, to the same purpose;

By reason of the strictness of the personal union, whatsoever may be verified of either of those natures (the divine or human) the same may be truly spoken of the whole person, from whethersoever of the natures it be denominated. And let him take in the other parts of that discourse with it, wherein he solidly proves that the Son of God took the nature of man (not an human person) into a personal union with himself, and so was manifest in flesh, and wrought our redemption; as also his pithy and pious discourse of this subject in his *Body of Divinity*, pg. 164, 165. &c. and it may prove of singular use to guide him out of that labyrinth of error he is at present lost in, if more gross tenets do not lie in the bottom of his discourses, than he is yet willing to speak out plainly before the world; which I would not suggest my suspicion of, did I not discern ground for it in what he hath already written, especially if compared with the heresies formerly espoused by him; but being willing to wait for his more plain and ingenuous opening of his own sense; I have for the present passed over many things, especially in his first chapter that are of an harsh sound in Christian ears, though clouded in ambiguous terms; expecting that his rejoinder will either give me occasion to put a better sense upon those phrases, than the words at present seem well to bear, or else engage me to a farther detection of his abomination couched in them.

With the latter part of Mr. Collier's book, which he entitles, *An Healing Word*,[2] I have not concerned myself, though divers things therein are liable to its just exception; but I must tell him, there can be no Gospel peace without truth, nor communion of saints, without an agreement in fundamental principles of the Christian religion. We must contend earnestly for the faith once delivered to the Saints; and mark those that cause divisions among us by their new doctrines contrary thereto, and avoid them; and lest any should be deceived by

---

[2] Thomas Collier, *A Healing Word* (London: Printed for the Author, 1676). It is bound with *The Additional Word*.

Mr. Collier's good words and fair speeches, I cannot but take notice that his general epistles were ushered into the world, with the same pretext of making peace, and discharge of his conscience, and with as great show of zeal for God, and other as plausible pretenses, as any he now maketh or can make; and yet one shall hardly find more contradictory and blasphemous notions, in the writings of any called, or pretending to be Christians, than in them: For, besides his contempt of the holy Scriptures, and all ordinances; there he tells us: "To have Communion and Fellowship with the Father, is to be one in Common with God; to have fellowship, is to be God's fellow; so is Christ, so are Saints," pg. 243, "Christ is no more than a Christian," pg. 244; with other like blasphemies, which I abhor the recital of. These things indeed (as I am informed) he saith he hath repented of; but never yet thought himself obliged to publish to the world an ingenuous recantation of them; that so those concerned might have from himself a plain and particular warning to take heed of that poison which hath flowed from his own pen: However, it may be a good warning to us not to heed the smooth, or swelling words of a man carried about with every wind of doctrine.

I have but a word or two more, and that is, to acquaint thee that I have been troubled for the delays that this little work hath met with, both before and since it went to the press, which yet I could not help; I have taken what care I could that errata in Printing it might be prevented, and desire that those παρόραματα,[3] which do occur, may be pardoned, and amended in reading (I hope they are not many, nor very material). And that thou mayest the sooner have a taste of the book I answer, I have in the following page given thee a specimen of Mr. Collier's strange heterodoxies collected out of his book (for the most part) in his own terms; which, with very many more contained therein, are detected and refuted in this. And give me leave to express my desires in the words of that holy man of old, concerning what I have written; *Domine Deus unus, Deus Trinitas; quæcunq; dixi in his*

---

[3] *"Errors, oversights."*

libris de tuo, agnoscant & tui; si qua de meo, & tu ignosce & tui; Amen!"[4] August.

Let God alone have the glory of anything serviceable to the interest of his truth in this treatise; and interpret well my poor essay towards the clearing thereof; much weakness therein I am sensible of; and know right well that one of deeper judgment, and greater abilities, endued with a more plentiful anointing of the good Spirit, would have said much more in less room than I have done: But seeing no other was engaged in this service, my mite is humbly offered; and that my weakness may be pardoned, and my poor endeavors succeeded to some advantage (if it be but of the weakest) of Christ's sheep, and the reflecting of some glory to his holy name, is the earnest prayer of,

The unworthiest of his servants,

N.C.

---

[4] "*O Lord the one God, God the Trinity, whatever I have said in these books that is of Thine, may they acknowledge who are Thine; if anything of my own, may it be pardoned both by Thee and by those who are Thine. Amen.*" Augustine, "On the Trinity" in Philip Schaff, ed. *Nicene and Post-Nicene Fathers* (Peabody: Hendrikson, 2004 reprint), III:228. These are the final words of Augustine's treatise.

Amongst the many gross errors published by Mr. Collier in his *Additional Word*, and refuted in this treatise, are these following:

1. That Christ is the Son of God only as considered in both natures. *Additional Word,* Ch. 1, pg. 2.
2. As he was the Prince of Life, the Lord of Glory, was he killed and crucified; and that was not in the human nature only, ch. 1, pg. 4.
3. As God-man he was a creature, ch. 1, pg. 9.
4. This creature God-man made all things, ch. 1, pg. 10.
5. The word God-man was made flesh, ch. 1, pg. 11.
6. There are Uncreated Heavens; for the eternal God must have some eternal habitation, ch. 1, pg. 12.
7. Christ died for the universe, the Heavens and Earth, and all things therein, ch. 2, pg. 13.
8. The Gospel ought to be preached to the whole creation, even to that part of it, that is not capable of hearing or understanding it, ch. 2, pg. 16.
9. The Foolish Virgins shall obtain some great privilege in the day of Christ, ch. 3, pg. 23.
10. Those that never heard the Gospel cannot be under the judgment of damnation, ch. 4, pg. 26.
11. The sinful defilement of our nature, is not the sin, but the affliction of man, ch. 4, pg. 26.
12. It's possible for men (in respect of power) to believe the Gospel, if God do not work at all upon them by his Spirit, ch. 5. pg. 31, 32.
13. Regenerate persons, or true believers, may finally fall away from God and perish, ch. 5, pg. 36, &c.

14. None shall be eternally damned but those that sin against the Holy Spirit, ch. 7, pg. 47.

15. The Gospel hath been preached to men after they were dead, ch. 7, pg. 48.

16. Men may repent so as to obtain deliverance from their torment, after death, and the last Judgment, ch. 7, pg. 48.

17. Sluggish Christians and formalists may find some mercy in the Day of Judgment, pg. 51.

18. Perhaps the torment of some sinners may not exceed a 100 years, pg. 52.

19. The Sodomites have already received their judgment, and are still suffering thereof, and the day of the general judgment is like to be their day of ease, pg. 53.

20. The infinite sacrifice of Christ remains the same, to have its influence for the obtaining of grace after the judgment as before, pg. 54.

CHAPTER I

Concerning God; The Distinct Subsistencies (*sic*) in the Divine Nature: and More Especially, the Person of the Son.

Mr. Collier intimates in the beginning of his first chapter, that he had been from some private hand admonished of certain errors by him before published in his *Body of Divinity*, which in this chapter he endeavors to vindicate; and makes this the occasion of the putting forth the whole of what we find in his *Additional Word*: But verily this course is in no wise like to give satisfaction to them who before were justly offended: For a man when he is blamed for swerving from the form of sound words, and that doctrine that is according to godliness in some instances; to repeat his errors with new confidence, instead of a retraction of them; and then to add many more, and more dangerous against the analogy of faith, yea the express words of Scripture, and common sentiments of all that deserve the name of Christians, is not the way to reconcile himself to the truth, or to any true lovers thereof: And that Mr. Collier hath thus done, will be manifested in our progress.

We are plentifully instructed from the Scripture, that there is but one only living and true God, who is a most pure spirit, eternal and immutable, incomprehensible, and infinitely perfect in his being, and all the properties thereof, &c.[1]

This also Mr. Collier professeth to own; yet he hath in the close of this first chapter of his *Additional Word*, dropped an expression or two that seem to hold no very full harmony therewith; He saith, pg. 12, "*As to the Omnipresence of God the Father, I say what the Scripture saith, which directeth us to the Father as in Heaven; and that by his Spirit he is present in all places.*"

Omnipresence is an essential property of God, grounded on his infiniteness; it is as necessary to him to be omnipresent, as to be God. It is all one therefore whether we speak of the omnipresence of the Father, or of the Son, or of the Holy Spirit, these three being that one incomprehensible and infinite Jehovah, to whom all fear and worship is due: And to deny it of any of them, is to deny their Divinity. And whereas Mr. Collier tells us, "*That he saith what the Scripture saith,*" &c. That is not enough, unless he make it manifest also, that he saith it according to the true sense and intendment of the Spirit of God in those Scriptures he refers unto. I am unwilling to entertain jealousies of any man; but yet I must say, that those Socinians who have most opposed the truth concerning the immensity of God, have yet said as much as Mr. Collier here presents us with; and to clear himself from suspicion in this matter when questioned about it, more might justly have been expected from him. The Scriptures indeed speak of God as in Heaven, but that is (as many other expressions in them are) in a way of condescension to our capacity. And we must always remember, that those things that are spoken of God ανθρωποπαθῶς[2] after the manner of men, must be interpreted θεοπρεπῶς[3] in a sense becoming God; else we must immediately close with, the gross and absurd

---

[1] This is the language of chapter two paragraph one of the Second London (1689) Confession.
[2] "*Anthropopathically.*"
[3] "*Proper to God.*"

heresies of the Anthropomorphites. Seeing then that we conceive of no place so glorious as Heaven, that is represented to us as the dwelling place, or throne of the Most High, that so we might be affected with his glorious majesty; Heaven also is the place where God doth manifest his Glory in a more eminent way than in any other part of the Creation: On these accounts, or some other like unto them, he is said to be in Heaven; but lest we should conceive of him as confined to any place, or limited in his being, we are expressly told in his word: "**The Lord your God, he is God in Heaven above, and in Earth beneath**," (Josh. 2.11). And again, "**Behold the Heavens, and the Heaven of Heavens cannot contain thee**," 1 Kings 8.27. "**Am I a God at hand saith the Lord, and not a God afar off? Can any hide himself in secret places that I shall not see him, saith the Lord? do not I fill Heaven and Earth, saith the Lord?**" (Jer. 23.24 with **Psalm 139**) and divers expressions of the same import we meet with therein, in other places. If then the Spirit of God be present in all places, the Father is so, and the Son is so, for the divine essence is undivided; and as I said at first, this is an essential property of God that we are speaking of. I might here stay to tell him in what a corrupt and impious sense some have used the expressions he here makes use of; but I shall proceed no farther with this point at present; if he declare himself to embrace the truth, this sufficeth; if he farther declare his mind in opposition thereto, we shall then have a fitter opportunity to enlarge on this head.

In the same page he doth reassert and endeavor to inforce his notion of the uncreated Heavens. But notwithstanding what he saith I cannot see how this notion may be reconciled, either with the Scripture, or right reason: Himself confesseth, that eternity is an attribute proper to God alone, and certainly to be uncreated is no less so: Creator and creature do divide all beings; how then can we conceive of any uncreated being but God himself, or of anything that is absolutely eternal besides himself? Again, if we allow him to conceive of an eternal and uncreated habitation for God; I ask him whether we may imagine any space without those Heavens: if not?

Then is the whole world within that uncreated and eternal dwelling place; which will hardly suit with Mr. Collier's opinion of it. If we may imagine space without those Heavens, then I ask whether we are to conceive of God in those Heavens, and not in that space; if he answer we are, then doth he indeed oppose the immensity and incomprehensibility of the holy one of Israel: If he say we are not to imagine him limited by these Heavens; then must he grant also, that he is everlastingly and essentially present, as well in the infinite space without them, as within them, for he is immutable; how then is the one his dwelling place more than the other? If Mr. Collier remove these, his notion may easily be clogged with other doubts: But we will consider what he offers for the proof thereof. Thus he pleads, pg. 12. §. 3: *"As for the uncreated Heavens, though in the term of uncreated it be not expressed, yet there is enough in Scripture to prove the truth thereof. For the eternal God must have some eternal habitation, as it is called in Isa. 57. 15. The high and holy place."*

    By Mr. Collier's own assertion (pg. 2 of his *Additional Word*) if he affirm that concerning the uncreated Heavens, which the Scriptures do not, it must needs be unsound and unsafe: He confesseth that in the term of uncreated they are not to be found in Scripture, but yet both here, and in his *Body of Divinity*, pg. 46, 47. he hath discovered the most glorious Heaven, such as the book of Job, or the Psalms make no mention of; for the Heavens, and the Heaven of Heavens mentioned therein, he affirms are polluted by the sin of man.

    And Mr. Collier doth intimate to his reader, as if the glory of the eternal God was not exalted above these most glorious Heavens; and that the Most High God doth not humble himself when he beholds them. As for the Heavens which were known to the Psalmist, and of which he speaks, Psalm 8.1, Psalm 113.4-6, Mr. Collier acknowledgeth God's glory to be set above all them, and that when he beholds them, he humbles himself; and hereof he gives you a double reason, viz. not only because he created them, (which is true) but also because as he affirms the created Heavens are all in a fallen estate, together with the

Earth, by reason of the sin of man: And therefore in his *Additional Word*, pg. 12 §. 5, he endeavors to prove the corruption of the Heavens by the sin of man, from Job 15.15: "**The Heavens are not clean in thy sight.**" But I conceive the scope of that text is by way of comparison, to show how vile man is, inasmuch as the purest part of the Creation, even the Heavens, *in conspectu Dei*,[4] or compared with the most holy pure God, are not to be reputed pure, rather than to impute to the Heavens any sinful defilement. So that here again we have another taste of Mr. Collier's unscriptural boldness: Whence doth he collect that the sin of man reached so high as to corrupt the Heavens? One would think, if there be any such corruption, it should rather be referred to the sin of angels, who were once inhabitants therein, than to the sin of man.

But to come to a more strict examination of his notion, concerning his supposed uncreated Heavens; which I take to be not only unscriptural, but anti-Scriptural; and his proof by his *oportet*[5] it must be so, to be most absurd and irrational.

The only text he quotes, upon which he would fasten his corrupt notion, is [Isa. 57.15][6], of which he takes only a part of a sentence, and omits the rest; the text speaks thus: "**For thus saith the high and holy one, that inhabiteth eternity, whose name is holy, I dwell in the high and holy place, with him also that is of a contrite and humble spirit, to revive the spirit of the humble, and to revive the heart of the contrite ones.**"

Here the habitation of the high and holy God is in general terms said to be in eternity, without reference to any place whatsoever; then he comes to distinguish of his present residence, and that is said to be, not only in the high and holy place (take it for Heaven), but withal, in the heart of every one of his humble and contrite saints: Heaven, and the heart of a believer, may be alike truly said, to be the habitation of God, Eph. 2.21-22. The Heaven of Heavens is not comprehensive

---

[4] "*In the sight of God.*"
[5] "*It must be so.*"
[6] The original text reads incorrectly "57:13."

of the immense God: Yet no believer's heart is too narrow for an habitation for him: And as the text doth express the high and holy place, and a contrite spirit on Earth, to be at the same instant God's dwelling place; so is it altogether silent as to this high and holy place, being uncreated.

But to manifest that Mr. Collier speaks not only without the Scriptures, but against the Scriptures herein, let these texts be considered:

"**Thus the Heavens were finished, and all the host of them**" (Gen. 2.1).

"**He commanded, and the Heaven of Heavens were created**" ([Psalm 148.4-5])[7].

"**By the word of the Lord were the Heavens made, and all the hosts of them**" (Psalm 33.6).

What the hosts of Heaven are, you may understand by 2 Chron. 18.18, Luke 2.13. And if these hosts of Heaven, the holy angels, do always behold the face of God: And all of them both place and inhabitants, were part of the six days creation; as Exod. 20.11. And if the face of God be beheld, where his glory is displayed in the greatest splendor, then certainly there is no color, nor place left for any uncreated Heavens.

And why cannot Mr. Collier conceive of the eternal God, without an eternal habitation distinct from himself? If he must have such an habitation, it is either because his happiness would not be perfect without it, which is to make him dependent on something beside himself, and to deny his Godhead, by denying his self-sufficiency: Or else it must be, because his being is such, as is determined and limited by certain bounds: as bodies are properly said to be in such or such a

---

[7] The original text reads incorrectly "48:4-5."

place; because they are circumscribed within some space that they fill up: Created spirits (though in a more improper sense), yet are truly said to be in a place; because, though they have not parts and dimensions as bodies have, so filling up the place where they are, nor can be punctually circumscribed as they may; yet they are so in some certain place, as not to be at the same time without it, or elsewhere. Now therefore when we conceive of the being of either of these, we must also conceive of some space susceptive of them, which we call "place," because they are finite: But what place can we conceive of for his dwelling therein, who is immense, and indistant to all places and things, present to all by and in his infinite essence and being, but contained in none? He adds:

> *"If God hath prepared a building, a house (for his people) not made with hands, eternal in the Heavens (2 Cor. 5.1), methinks it should be no crime to say that he hath an eternal habitation for himself, suitable to his name and nature, and if eternal then uncreated."*

I suppose the ambiguity of the word "**eternal,**" which Mr. Collier meets with in the text, is the occasion of his mistake in part; if we look into the Scriptures, we shall find mention made of a three-fold duration;

1. That which is absolutely eternal, without beginning or end; and this is proper to God alone.

2. That which hath a beginning but shall have no end, which for distinction sake is commonly called Æviternity. And

3. That which hath a beginning and shall have an end, which is time.

Now the term "**eternal**" is indifferently used in the Scripture to signify either of the two former; but this ambiguity is easily removed, if we consider the subject spoken of; when it is applied to God, we must take it in the first sense; but when unto creatures, in the second: So then the Apostle, as is clear from the scope of the text, when he speaks of an "**house eternal**" in the Heavens, doth not intend a building that had been from everlasting, but such an one as notwithstanding its creation (for it was made, though without hands, by the power of God) in time, should not decay as the earthly house of our tabernacle doth, but abide incorruptible forever. And let not Mr. Collier think, that because we need a house, a building in the Heavens to complete our happiness; that therefore the former of all things doth so. So then this text will not bear the weight he lays on it: And when in the close he infers from the eternity of God's dwelling place, that it is also "*uncreated,*" he might have added, "and then God;" for this necessarily follows upon the grant of the other: And by this very medium Mr. Collier in his *Body of Divinity*, pg. 85 proves, that angels are created beings: His words are these: "*Reason teacheth that they must be and are created, or else they must be eternal, which is proper to none but God; and if so they must be God; but they are not God,*" &c.

And by that Mr. Collier may see that he hath entangled himself in meddling with things that he understands not. But I shall proceed;

The Scripture doth also instruct us concerning the subsistence of God, or the manner of his being; and this is such a glorious mystery as by his word only is revealed to us; we cannot by reason comprehend it, but ought to adore it; and by faith rest in his testimony concerning it.

In 1 John 5.7 we are taught, that there are three that do subsist in the divine essence; and that these three are the Father, the Word, and the Spirit, who are the one true God. Here then is set before us the divine essence, subsisting in three relative properties:

> The relative property of the Father is to beget (Psalm 2.7; John 3.16).

The relative property of the Son is to be begotten;
The relative property of the Holy Spirit is to be breathed, or to proceed from the Father and the Son (John 15.26; Rom. 8.9; &c).

Now unto these relative properties belong all imaginable perfection; but no imperfection, because they are in God: Therefore as considered in him they do infer personality, because a personal subsistence, is the most perfect manner of being in the whole reasonable nature: And throughout the Scriptures when the Father, Son, or Holy Ghost are distinctly spoken of, those terms are made use of that are proper only unto a person; and personal operations are everywhere ascribed to them; though in our conception of personality in the Divine nature, we must separate from it whatsoever imperfection is seen in a created person: Every created person hath a limited essence distinct and distant one from another: But all the uncreated persons in the deity have the same immense undivided essence, and are the one eternal immortal invisible only wise God. In created persons also there is difference of time in the proceeding of one from the other, but here though there be an eternal order of origination, there is no priority of time or nature. Add hereunto the warranty of this term from Heb. 1.3, where it is applied to the Father (and there is the same reason for our using it, when we speak of the Son or Spirit), and I cannot see why Mr. Collier should reject or except against it as he doth, pg. 11, 12, and in his *Body of Divinity*. However I shall not strive about words, if the thing be owned: But it is commonly seen, that men have been offended with apt terms, because the things expressed by them have been displeasing to them. But I shall pass this also, and return to the beginning of his chapter, that his strange notions about the person of the Son of God may be brought to examination.

And that I may proceed with the more clearness, I will first briefly represent what the Scripture teacheth in this matter.

That the Son of God might become the author of eternal

salvation unto lost sinners, he took upon him the office of a Mediator betwixt God and them; and in order to the accomplishment of what he had undertaken on their behalf, it was necessary that he should take hold of their nature, and be manifested in flesh. In the person of Christ therefore we are to mind,

1. The distinction of both natures, divine and human.

2. The union of both natures in the person of the Mediator.

First, both the divine and human nature in Christ remain distinct in their essence, and all their essential properties, and necessarily must do so, the one being created, and the other uncreated; the divine nature cannot be changed into the human, nor the human into the divine; neither is it possible that they should be so confounded or mixed together, as to make a third nature distinct from both. "**The Word was God, and the Word was made flesh**" (John 1). "**He was in the form of God, and yet took upon him the form of a servant**" (Phil. 2). He was and remained the only begotten of the Father, his own Son, and yet was in all things made like to us, sin only excepted. He was true God: God by nature, and true man also, made of the seed of David, as concerning the flesh.

Secondly, there is a glorious and unspeakable union of both natures in the person of Christ: As he is Immanuel he is but one person, and as such is spoken of throughout the Scripture; even the same person that in the beginning was with God: The human nature of Christ never having a personality of its own, did from the first moment of its being subsist in the person of the Son of God.[8] So then,

---

[8] In the margin next to this sentence is the note: "Vid. *Amesii Medullam*," or, "see Ames's Marrow." The reference is to Guilielmum Amesium, *Medulla S.S. Theologiae* (London: Robertum Allotium, 1630), the Latin original which was subsequently translated as William Ames, *The Marrow of Sacred Divinity* (London: Henry Overton, 1642). Ames (1576-1633) was an important English puritan theologian exiled in Europe. See Keith Sprunger, *The Learned Doctor William Ames* (Urbana: The University of Illinois Press, 1972).

1. Though the second person of the deity have but one only subsistence, yet his subsistence is to be considered with a twofold respect; first, as he was in the divine nature from eternity; and also as he was manifest in the flesh; which last infers no change in God, but only a relation: The Son of God remained what he was; although he became what he was not, by uniting the human nature with the divine in one person.

2. Though there is not, nor cannot be a real transfusion of the properties of the divine nature into the human, or of the human into the divine, yet by reason of this strict union of both natures, there is a personal communication of properties, which doth consist in a communion or concurrence of both natures unto the same operations, so as they are done by both natures together, yet each nature worketh according to its own properties: So that all that Christ did or suffered, is properly referred to his person: but if we consider the immediate principle of his actions, some of them must be referred to his divine nature only, others to his human.

3. Hence ariseth, and herein is sounded, that communication of properties in the Scriptures speaking of Christ;

    1. When that is spoken of the person that agreeth to him only with respect to one of his natures; as when Christ is said to die, of which he was capable only in his human nature, or to create all things which was proper to his divine nature. And sometimes it is said of him, that "**he knew what was in man,**" that "**he searcheth the reins,**" &c. at another time, that "**he knew not the Day of Judgment:**" So likewise of God it is true, that he cannot be tempted of evil; and yet Christ, who was God as well as man, suffered being tempted; but then this could not be as God, but as man, considered as made like to his brethren in all things, except

sin: Neither can we avoid contradiction, without embracing this way of exposition, which is alone suited to the mind of the Spirit of God in such sayings; and founded in the real distinction of both natures, without division in the person of Christ.

2. Sometimes also that is attributed to one nature (as it doth connote the person) that is proper to the other, so Acts 20.28, and 1 John 3.16. That is spoken of God, viz. his shedding his blood, and laying down his life; which cannot without blasphemy be affirmed of the divine nature as such.

3. And again, that which is only proper to the person as such, considered in both natures, is attributed to the one nature; as 1 Tim. 2.5, "**There is one Mediator betwixt God and men, the man Christ Jesus.**" He was not Mediator as man only, nor as God only, but as God-man in one person.

These things well weighed, may deliver us from that strange confusion that Mr. Collier's discourse tends to cast us into, and might serve for a refutation of his first chapter; but for the help of the weak (for whose sake this work was undertaken) I will particularly examine whatever therein might be occasion of stumbling to them, and remove it out of the way.

In pg. 1 of his book he thus writes,

The exceptions against what I said in this matter (i.e. relating to the person of the Son of God) are as followeth,

1. That he is not the Son of God in the divine nature only.

2. That he is the Son of God only as considered in both natures.

> *3. That he was the Word as he was God-man and man-God.*
>
> *4. That as God-man he was a creature.*
>
> *5. That this creature God and man created all things.*
>
> *6. That this Word God-man was made flesh.*
>
> *7. That he is the Son of Man in both natures.*

By these words of his one would conclude these gross contradictions, were the assertions of the animadverter[9] on his book; but his meaning is, that these are the things excepted against in it, which he still owns, and undertakes the vindication of them, in which fruitless attempt I shall attend him; He begins with the first:

> *That he is not the Son of God in the Divine nature only. My reason for this is, because the Scripture nowhere (that I know) affirms him so to be, and for me or any other to affirm, that which the Scripture doth not, must needs be unsound and unsafe: The Scripture always when it speaks of the Son of God, it is as he was in both natures, God and Man; and hence it is safe to say, that he was not the Son of God in the Divine nature only.*

Had I met with this position concerning Christ by itself, that "*he is not the Son of God in the Divine nature only,*" charity would have moved me to hope, that the design thereof (though the words are harsh and improper) had been no more than to assert the indissoluble union of the human nature with the divine, in one person, since the incarnation of the Son of God. But his defense thereof, together with his following positions, will in no wise admit this sense, but determine his meaning to be that "*Christ is no otherwise (nor ever was) the Son of God, but as he was God-man, considered in both natures.*" Whence it

---

[9] The critic.

necessarily followeth, that either he had no existence before the days of Augustus Caesar, when he was born of a virgin; or else that he had both natures, and was a man, before he came of the seed of David as concerning the flesh: And this last absurdity he seems not to stick at in his following lines. The argument he endeavors to confirm his notion by, may thus be framed:

> That which the Scripture nowhere affirms, is unsound and unsafe for any man to affirm.
> But the Scripture nowhere affirms Christ to be the Son of God in the divine nature only.
> Ergo, for any man to affirm it is unsound and unsafe.

If his meaning in his first proposition be, that every notion that is not either expressed in terms in the Scripture, or by just consequence deduced from it (for *ex veris nil nisi verum*[10]) is unsound, we grant it; but then his assumption is false and must be denied: All the inforcement he gives it is in these words, "*The Scripture always when it speaks of the Son of God, it is as he was in both natures God and Man.*" But I shall prove the contrary by an instance or two (out of those many that might be produced) from the Scripture.

The first is Psalm 33.6 "**By the word of the Lord were the Heavens made.**" This text I do the rather mention, because Mr. Collier confesseth, pg. 2, that it is the Son of God that is here spoken of under the name of the Word; and it is evident, that he is not here spoken of as he was God-man; but only as he did subsist in the form of God: The design of the Psalmist being to set forth the glory of his eternal power and God-head, by enumerating some of his great works, in this and the following verses. As he is the Creator of all things is his praise here celebrated, long before he became Immanuel by taking our nature.

---

[10] Coxe later explains this phrase: "The just and necessary consequence of a true notion, is truth, and nothing else." A literal translation with implied words in square brackets would be: *"from true [things] nothing [comes] except [that which is] true."*

The next Scripture I urge for the proof of Christ's being spoken of as the Son of God before his Incarnation, is Proverbs 8, from v. 22 to the end of the chapter. Which text hath always been a grievous eyesore to the enemies of the Son of God; and hath by the Orthodox been pleaded with great advantage, both against the Arians, and Socinians. The last mentioned have laid in all the cavils they could devise, to persuade men that it is not the Son of God that is here intended; and with them Mr. Collier joins, and puts in his exceptions also against the application of it to him, pg. 7. The learned know where and by whom this text with others, have been fully vindicated from their exceptions; and amongst others Dr. Owen in his *Exercitations* prefixed to the second part of his *Exposition of the Hebrews*, pg. 37,[11] &c. hath so learnedly and solidly asserted the truth by me pleaded for, from this text; with so full an answer to all Socinian cavils against it, as leaves no ground for Mr. Collier's saying *"That it is a question too hard for any man to resolve, whether this Scripture intend the Son of God or not."* His fond trifling in the exposition of it, I shall not trouble myself with, but only remove his exceptions laid in against the true sense of it; which being established, his gloss upon it vanisheth without farther trouble.

That an intelligent person is intended in this text, almost every verse in the chapter doth confirm, for all kind of personal properties are ascribed to it; and if we compare this with ch. 1, v. 21, *ad finem*;[12] we must acknowledge, that Wisdom speaking in them is a person, and a divine person too, unto whom all fear and obedience is due; or else there is no such mentioned in the Scripture. Moreover Christ is expressly called Wisdom in the New Testament (Matt. 11.19; 1 Cor. 1.30), and the word there, is of the feminine gender as well as here; which evidenceth the vanity of that cavil of Mr. Collier, *"That Christ*

---

[11] John Owen, *Exercitations on the Epistle to the Hebrews Concerning the Person of Christ* (London: Nathaniel Ponder, 1674). John Owen (1616-1683), pastor, scholar, expositor and theologian should need no introduction. See Crawford Gribben, *John Owen and English Puritanism* (Oxford: OUP, 2017).

[12] The original text reads "chap. 1.21." *Ad finem* means *"to the end."*

is not intended, because the Wisdom here spoken of is in the feminine gender." What terms can express at once the whole of his glory who is infinite? Neither is there anything here spoken of Wisdom, that is not in other Scriptures attributed to Christ: As we may see in a brief parallel, v. 22: "**The Lord possessed me in the beginning of his way,**" &c. John 1, "**In the beginning was the Word.**" Verse 23: "**I was set up from everlasting,**" &c. Mic. 5.2, "**Whose going forth have been from of old, from everlasting.**" So 2 Tim. 1.9, grace is said to be given us "**in Christ before the world began.**" Verse 25: "**Before the mountains were settled, before the hills I was brought forth:**" [Col. 1.15],[13] 17: He is "**the first born of every creature, and before all.**" Verses 29, 30: "**When he appointed the foundations of the earth, then I was by him:**" John 1.2, "**And the Word was in the beginning with God.**" "**I was daily his delight, rejoicing always before him:**" Matt. 3.17, "**This is my beloved Son in whom I am well pleased:**" Verse 32: "**Now therefore hearken unto me O ye children:**" Matt. 17.5, "**Hear ye him.**" Thus I might pass through the whole context, but this sufficeth at present; Mr. Collier still objecteth, *"That here is no mention of the Son under that name and title."* That Christ is not here called the Son of God in terms, doth not in the least weaken the testimony of this Scripture, seeing it is manifest that such a person is here spoken of as can be no other than the Son of God; and the relative property of the second subsistence in the divine nature is so expressly mentioned, that it is abundantly evident he is here spoken of as the Son of God before time: This we find first, v. 22: "**The Lord possessed me [**קנני**]**[14] **in the beginning of his ways:**" The word signifies either to acquire something, or to possess it being acquired: Now amongst other ways of acquiring, acquisition, and so possession by right of paternity or generation, is

---

[13] The original text reads incorrectly "2:15."
[14] *"He (Yahweh) acquired me"* or *"he (Yahweh) possessed me."*

one: so the same word is used in Gen. 4.2[15] and as the circumstances of the text do necessitate us to embrace that sense here, so the following words do put it out of doubt; for thus he proceeds, v. 24: **"When there were no deeps was I brought forth:"** And again v. 25: **"Before the hills I was brought forth."** The word is the same in both places [חוללתי][16] which is in like manner by many learned interpreters rendered **"brought forth,"** (Psalm 51.5). So then here is the eternal generation of the person spoken of: In that it is from everlasting it can be applicable to none, but he that is God by nature; and in that it is to be **"begotten"** or **"brought forth"** that is here predicate of him; it can be no other than the divine nature subsisting in the incommunicable property of a Son, that is here spoken of; and an illustrious exposition of these words you have John 1.1 &c. But Mr. Collier saith, "*The word translated 'brought forth,' is in the Hebrew 'formed,' else he could not be set up from everlasting.*" That the Hebrew word ought to be rendered "*formed*," he offers not to prove; and his saying so, doth not at all inforce it: Nay, either he is unacquainted with that language (which is very probable) and took this by hearsay from some Arian, or else he doth wittingly impose upon his ignorant reader, that cannot contradict him. The root from whence that word comes, viz. חול doth properly signify the pain and sorrow of a woman in travail:[17] *Peculiare est parturientium; nisumq; parturiendi proprie significat.*[18] Mercer. And hence being formed in Piel,[19] it signifies

---

[15] Although Coxe cites Gen 4:2, he is actually referring to Gen 4:1, where the previously stated Hebrew word also occurs in Eve's statement, "I have acquired a man with *the aid* of Yahweh." The name of Cain, the man acquired, is a play on this Hebrew word.

[16] "*I was brought forth (through labor).*"

[17] The root form could also have been חיל. In either case, this Hebrew verb, used in Prov 8:24-25 and elsewhere, frequently describes the travail of labor and delivery. (cf. Deut 32:18; Job 15:7; 39:1; Ps 29:9; 51:7; Isa 51:2; 66:8 of the Masoretic Text.)

[18] "*It is particularly of pregnant [women]; and it properly means the labour of giving birth.*" The quotation may be found in Iacobi Bolduci, Commentaria in Librum Iob (Parisiorum: 1619), 637, but Mercer is not cited as a source, while Montanus and Pagninus (see the following footnote) are cited in the margin. The work by Mercer has not been identified; see below on Mercer.

[19] Also called a Polel with a hollow verb like חיל.

properly to cause to bring forth, or to bring into the pain attending parturition, so it is used, Psalm 29.9, and in Pual,[20] as it is formed here, it can signify no other thing than "**to be brought forth**;" according to its proper import: It is granted that from hence it sometimes borroweth other significations, as from the grief of parturition, it is transferred to signify any sorrow or grief: And because the product of art in forming something, is a kind of birth, or bears some similitude to it, being oft accomplished not without care and pain, which also bear some similitude unto the pains of parturition; it is sometimes transferred to signify the "formation of a thing by art or otherwise." But this is a sure rule, that the proper signification of a word is to be retained, unless the circumstances of the text, or the analogy of faith require the contrary. But both favor, yea necessitate this sense in this place; it is impious to think, that he which claims religious worship to himself, as Wisdom doth in the close of the chapter, is a formed creature only. Mr. Collier adds, if it be not so, "*he could not be set up from everlasting*;" this doth not at all weaken, but inforce what I have pleaded: Divers able interpreters, viz. Pagn. Mont. Merc. Vatabl.,[21] read it, "I obtained a principality, or was constituted a prince from everlasting:" The intendment of these words we have fully expressed: Col. 1.15-16 with Heb. 1.2. The Son is Lord of the whole Creation, and heir of all things; and this right of

---

[20] Also called a Polal with a hollow verb like חיל.

[21] These authors are: Pagn: Santes Pagninus, 1470-1536, a Dominican disciple of Savonorola; see J. D. Douglas, ed. *New International Dictionary of the Christian Church* (Grand Rapids: Zondervan, 1974), 742; Mont: Benedictus Arias Montanus: Orientalist, exegete, editor of Antwerp Polyglot, died 1598; see Charles G. Herbermann et. al., *The Catholic Encyclopedia* (New York: Robert Appleton, 1907), I:711; Merc: Joannes Mercerus or Jean Mercier: d. 1570. Pupil and successor of Francois Vatable at College Royal, Paris, 1546. Published works on Hebrew and Semitic grammar; Latin translations and editions of Targums; Bible commentaries; Beza published his commentary on Genesis in Geneva in 1598. See Scott Manetsch, ed. *Reformation Commentary on Scripture: 2 Corinthians* (Downers Grove: InterVarsity, 2022), 453; Vatabl: Francois Vatablus (Vatable), Hebraist and theologian. Taught at the College de France in Paris and was appointed Abbot of Bellozane by Francis I. See Philip Schaff, ed., *The New Schaff Herzog Encyclopedia of Religious Knowledge* (New York: Funk and Wagnells, 1912), 12:143.

principality in him hath a double foundation;

1. It is in him as he is the Son begotten of the substance of the Father, having the same essence with him, and the Creator of all things.

2. It is founded in the Covenant of Redemption made between the Father and him, and is referred to his mediatory kingdom: The first belongs to him by necessity of nature from everlasting, unto his mediatory kingdom and principality he was designed of God according to Covenant, and foreordained from everlasting. There is then nothing in these words that will give Mr. Collier any relief; what he farther adds, requires no answer: So then here is a second witness to the everlasting Sonship of Christ, before he was God-man.

I will mention one text more, where we have not only the thing, but even the term plainly expressed, Prov. 30.4—"**Who hath established all the ends of the Earth? What is his name, or what is his Son's name, if thou canst tell?**" This Scripture fully holds forth, that the Father had a Son before the Incarnation of Christ, whose name was Wonderful, and his glory as unspeakable as that of the Father; it is therefore the Son of God, not as made flesh, but as he was from eternity with God, having his essence and glory that is here mentioned.

But why do I stay to enumerate particular testimonies? Seeing all those Scriptures that speak of his divine nature do confirm the truth pleaded for, John 1: "**The Word was God, and the Word was made flesh**;" How and when he was made flesh, the other Evangelists particularly relate: But before that, this Word was in the beginning with God, and he is acknowledged by Mr. Collier to be the second in the Trinity, and that this title is the Son. And indeed the being of the divine essence is not more necessary, than the manner of its being, i.e. the incommunicable relative properties thereof, or the subsisting of the Father, Son, and Holy Spirit therein.

I conclude therefore, that it is not only safe and sound to assert, but moreover that it always was an article of the common faith of Christians, that the Son of God *was*, before he was made flesh, while he subsisted only in the form of God; and to deny that he was the Son of God in the divine nature only, is by just consequence to deny that he hath a divine nature, seeing it either infers an utter denial of his pre-existence to his Incarnation, or at least, that the nature he had before, was neither person nor Son, until it received its perfection, and became both by the uniting of the human nature thereto.

By Mr. Collier's after-discourse it appears, that he hath been cast upon those absurd contradictions that this chapter is filled with, by a very gross mistake of the Decree of God concerning Christ, and the prophecies of his coming in the flesh: Because it was from eternity decreed that the Son of God should become Immanuel, he concludes, that he is to be considered as being actually God-man from everlasting; and because it was foretold what he should be, therefore he always was such an one. But he may as well conclude, that himself, or any other thing that ever was, is, or shall be in nature, had an everlasting existence, seeing the futurition of all these, was from everlasting determined in God's Decree.

Having thus removed the foundation of his whole discourse on this subject, I shall not trouble the reader with a reply to every [futile][22] cavil and contradiction I meet with in the remaining part of this chapter, but pass through it with all speed and brevity.

He proceeds to the second position, which depends on the first, viz. that "*he is the Son of God only as considered in both natures.*"

His reason for this is the same also in effect with his former, and his whole plea in defense of it, is already sufficiently enervated: But because he here endeavors to wrest many texts, to countenance his notion, I will in few words reply to his abuse of them. The first is John 1.2 & 14. Let that whole context be soberly considered, and we need

---

[22] Original reads "futilious."

no more to reprove Mr. Collier's folly. But he saith, "*The Scriptures that speak of Christ as in the bosom of the Father before time, speak of him as he came forth in time.*"

That the Son of God, as to his divine nature, "**is the same yesterday, today, and forever,**" is certain; and that the Godhead of Christ underwent no change when he was made flesh, is before proved: But that he took not into a personal union with himself a nature he had not before, when he was made flesh, is false and absurd; and directly opposeth the very terms of the text produced by him.

Indeed it is too evident that Mr. Collier doth not understand the force of the particle "as," which he so frequently useth; and therefore he supposeth, that whatsoever is spoken of the person that was God-man, is indifferently spoken of either nature as such in that person. Whereas (although the body and soul of man do make up but one human nature) in ordinary discourse we hear those things attributed to that person who is both animal and rational, of which some belong to him only as he is animal, viz. to eat, drink, sleep, die; others only as he is rational, viz. to understand, deliberate, will, &c. It is to be bewailed that a man which stumbles at such things as these, should become troublesome to the world by printing his impertinencies.

The next Scripture insisted on by him is Rom. 8.29, unto which we may add Eph. 1.4; 1 Tim. 1.9. Mr. Collier's reasonings from these Scriptures is to this purpose,

> *God did choose and bless his people in Christ before the world was, even in Christ the anointed who is the Son of God, and was then with the Father. But he is not Christ in the divine nature only, nor in the human nature only, but as God-man. Therefore as God-man he was with the Father before time, and as such only is his Son.*

It is true that God did never intend the salvation of any sinners but in and by Christ, and when God did before time choose a remnant in him, he had a respect to his Incarnation, and redeeming of them according to the terms of the Covenant between the Father and Christ: They were chosen then in Christ considered as one that had undertaken to be a mediator betwixt God and men, and in order to the accomplishing of what he so undertook, in the fullness of time to become Immanuel, the Messiah, or anointed of the Lord; it is true also that Christ is the Son of God: But that he is so as the Christ, and could not have been so unless he had been our savior, or that he was anointed to be the Son of God, and was not so by nature, is impious and false. So likewise to conceit that he was actually God-man, when we were chosen in him, as Mr. Collier doth, can arise from no other ground, but his confounding the Decree of God with the execution thereof. And let but the reader compare Phil. 2 referred to by him with 1 Pet. 1.20, with which he closeth this section, and he will need no other antidote against Mr. Collier's doctrine.

The next series of texts abused by him, are these wherein we have prediction of Christ's coming in the flesh; divers of which he cites, pg. 3, and concerning them he saith,

> "*The Scriptures that foretell of him before he was come in the flesh, so speak of him as to come, viz. God and man,*" &c.

If there be any kind of argument in that section, it must be this (which to recite is to confute),

> *The Scriptures that foretell Christ's coming in the flesh, speak of the Son of God.*
> *But they foretell that the Messiah should be God-man, ergo,*
> *He is the Son of God only as considered in both natures.*

I might answer as pertinently as he argues, *Si placet Domine negatur applicatio*[23] (as a young scholar once replied to his tutor). It is strange that a man who undertakes to teach others, should yet himself

---

[23] "*If it pleases, Lord, the application is denied.*"

be to learn to distinguish between predictions and their fulfilling; he finds it foretold that the Son of God should be incarnate, ergo he always was so. But it is just with God to leave men to such absurdities in undertakings of this kind as Mr. Collier is now engaged in.

He proceeds, pg. 4, 5, to reckon up many of those texts, that speak of the birth of Christ, his converse with men in the days of his Flesh, his Death, Resurrection, and Session at the right hand of God; all which are cleared, and his exceptions removed, by that which I laid down in my entry upon this point, whither I refer the reader: Desiring him to remind Rom. 9.5 with other texts of like import that frequently occur in the New Testament. I know Mr. Collier scornfully rejects what I insist on, in his eighth page, but offers no reason for his so doing; and the contradiction, yea blasphemy that he runs upon in refusing that truth, may warn us to give the more heed thereto. Thus he writes pg. 4, § 5, "*And as he was the Prince of Life, Acts 3.15, the Lord of Glory, 1 Cor. 2.8, was he killed and crucified, and certainly that was not in the human nature only; for so he could not be the Prince of Life and Lord of Glory.*" I wish Mr. Collier had seriously thought of that saying, **Add thou not unto his words lest he reprove thee, and thou be found a liar** (Prov. 30.6). In the Scriptures cited by him there is no such thing written, "*that as he was the Prince of Life, &c. he was killed and crucified:*" They say indeed, that the Prince of Life was killed, and the Lord of Glory was Crucified: So the Scripture saith also, that God purchased his Church by his blood; and laid down his life for us: The person that died was very God, the Prince of Life and Lord of Glory, but it was in his human nature, and not in his divine that he suffered, although both made but one person; and to reject this, and say with Mr. Collier, that as God &c. his blood was shed, he was crucified and died, i.e. that all these things befell the divine as well as the human nature; is impious to that degree, as may make a tender heart bleed, and the ears of a godly man to tingle. He saith in the same section,

"*That unscriptural notion doth not reach the case, that the human nature satisfied; it is the same who suffered, that satisfied.*" The common faith of Christians about this matter is, that the same Jesus who suffered made satisfaction to divine justice for their sins; but that his sufferings were in his human nature only, and the worth of them for satisfaction to justice did arise from the union of the human nature with the divine in one person; so that the Godhead of Christ put an infinite value into his sufferings. This he offers not to disprove; and they have taken it up on better grounds than to part with it, because he boldly censures it as an unscriptural notion.

In pg. 5 &c. Mr. Collier doth also undertake to give answer to some texts produced to prove that Christ was the Son of God in the divine nature; the first is John 10.30,

> *I and my Father are one, that is (say they), one in the same substance, &c. And a little after, that Christ did not intend himself to be the Son of God in the divine nature only is apparent; because he speaks of himself as he was the Son of God, not as he was not, viz. as he was God and man visible, and not of the divine nature only which was invisible, and must have been an unseen Son, which could not be understood.*

This text doth fully prove that Christ hath the same essence with the Father, and therefore (without respect to his being made flesh) was from everlasting begotten of the substance of the Father; and this generation is the foundation of that relative property of a Son, in which he did subsist before the world was. This we say, and other texts do so fully assert it, and manifest its lying in the foundation of the Christian religion, that I will not doubt to say he is an heretic that doth deny it. In the following reasoning of Mr. Collier it is evident he miserably begs the question; "*it cannot*," he saith, "*intend his Sonship in the divine nature, because in that only he was not the Son of God.*" But this he should have proved, not dictated against the testimony produced. What he saith of the invisibility of the Son in the divine nature, may be as well applied to the denial of the subsisting of the Father, or Holy Spirit, who also are the invisible God. And Mr. Collier can never prove that it is necessary unto the being of the Son of God, that he should be visible. The other texts minded by him do (divers of them) speak expressly of a person sent into the world in our nature; which was the Son of God; and in that he is called the Son of God, when found in fashion as a man; it doth firmly prove the personal union of both natures in him; but not in the least intimate, that he was not a Son, before he was a man, as Mr. Collier would seduce his readers to believe. And this may suffice to this head also.

His third position is, "*That he was the Word as God-man and man-God,*" or as he explains it, pg. 8, "*That the same Word and Son of God, God-man was made flesh,*" &c. which falls in with his 6th position, pg. 11.

How abundantly the Scriptures hold forth a distinction, betwixt the Word that took human nature, and the nature assumed by him, hath been already manifested; and that the Word was from everlasting with God, and was God, the human nature not so. And the absurdity of his 6th thesis is obvious even to a child; what was it for the Word to be made flesh, but to become a man; and if he was God-man from everlasting, how could he be made a man in time? The truth is, Mr. Collier fairly intimates his good-will to deny Christ's coming of the seed of David as concerning the flesh; for in answer to this objection he saith, pg. 11, "*He that was God and man in God's eye, was made so in our eye, when made or manifested in flesh:*" So then he was a man before, it seems, only we knew it not; and his human nature he took not of the virgin, but brought it from Heaven with him? If this be not his sense, he speaks nothing to the purpose; and if it be, I desire he would speak out in his next, and the abomination of it shall be farther detected. For the present he produceth nothing more that may give any seeming countenance to these notions, or in the least free them from the highest absurdity; I shall leave them therefore naked, as they are proposed by him, and follow him to his fourth thesis.

"*That as God-man he was a creature,*" i.e. He was a creature as God, as well as in his human nature. Verily Mr. Collier may as well persuade us, that the creature is God, as that God is a creature. I will not suppose his reader or mine, to be utterly brutish and without understanding, and therefore shall leave this idle and contradictious fiction to confute itself also. Only I will add an exposition of Col. 1.15, abused by him, pg. 10, where he falls in directly with the notion of the Arian heretics; and would persuade us, "*That if Christ be not here considered as the first-born of every creature as being one of them, there is nothing in the text.*" But the contrary is abundantly manifested by Dr. Owen in his answer to Biddle the Socinian his catechism, from whence I shall transcribe enough to stop Mr. Collier's mouth, and to inform those that have not that treatise by them. Observe then,

Although in the 15, 16, and 17 verses the Apostle speaks of him who is the mediator (God-man), yet he speaks not of him as mediator, but that he enters upon v. 18. But,

> *His present design being to set forth the excellent glory of Christ, he speaks of those things that appertain to him as God: For,*

The Creation of all things by him is more emphatically expressed, v. 16, together with the end of their creation; they were created by him and for him, he is the heir of all things: and in v. 17, his preexistence unto all things, and his providence in supporting them, and continuing that being to them which he gave them is asserted. And on this account, for this reason is he said to be the "**first-born of every creature**;" which are the words Mr. Collier cavils at; he therefore by whom all things, all creatures were created, is none of them, otherwise he must create himself: He is said to be πρωτότοκος πάσης κτίσεως, not πρωτόκτισος the first-born,[24] not the first created, that is the Prince, Heir, and Lord of the whole creation, so that his privilege, rule, and inheritance of and over all creatures is here expressed, which suits the Apostle's aim, to set out the excellency of Christ above all

---

[24] "*First born of every creature*" not "*first created.*"

creatures. His being begotten is opposed to the creation of all things. First in the Scripture is sometimes used with respect to things going before, in which sense it denies all order or series of things in the same kind; so God is said to be the first, Isa. 41.4. "**Because before him there is none**" (Isa. 43.11). And in this sense is Christ the first born, so the first born as to be the only begotten Son of God. He is also said to be the beginning of the creation of God, because he giveth, and continueth being to all creatures. And whereas Mr. Collier saith he is a "*creature and the Creator too;*" we grant it; but not *secundum idem*,[25] in the same nature. As he was God he is the Creator, as man a creature.

He saith farther in the 5th place,

"That this creature God-man made all things."

As God-man he is not a mere creature: It is true Christ made all things, as we saw in the preceding text, but not as man, for he was made flesh long after, but when he subsisted only in the form of God, long before he was a creature. His 6th position is answered before.

He adds 7thly, that "*he is the Son of Man in both natures.*"

As to his human nature, and that only he was made of the seed of David: But the union of both natures, was so strict and indissoluble in the person of Christ, that it is truly said, that holy thing that was born of the virgin was the Son of God. The person who as to his human nature was formed of the seed of the virgin, being God's ἴδιος υἱος[26] his proper Son begotten of his own substance from everlasting, as to his divine nature. And this distinction of natures in Christ strictly observed, doth not at all infer a plurality of persons or sons, as Mr. Collier vainly imagines, pg. 8, in his question: For the human nature hath no subsistence of its own; it is the same person who is the Son of God and the Son of David, yet is he the Son of God in his divine nature in contradistinction from the human, and the Son of David with respect to our nature that he took of the virgin in contradistinction

---

[25] "*According to the same [nature].*"
[26] "*Proper son.*"

from the divine nature; though these natures since the Incarnation, cannot possibly be divided or separated. And if this be not owned, we must bring in a confusion of natures in the person of Christ.

As to what he adds about Justification, it shall be taken notice of in a more convenient place.

Whereas Mr. Collier closeth his chapter with an affirmation, that "*he cannot yet be convinced of anything written in his Body of Divinity* [wherein himself owneth these things are found] *of which he yet seeth cause to repent.*" Truly his blindness renders him an object of pity. And because he supposeth these strange heterodoxies have proceeded from his being enriched in knowledge beyond all others, his case is the more dangerous. But oh that he would be advised to go to Christ for eye-salve that he might see; and then we should hear another story from him.

While I was engaged in my answer to Mr. Collier, I received from the hand of a friend some animadversions on this chapter of his, especially respecting his second position concerning the person of Christ; which because they are not long, and may give some farther light into this matter under debate, I have here annexed.

Mr. Collier's *Additional Word*, pg. 2,

> *That which I shall endeavor to demonstrate from Scripture is, that he is the Son of God only as considered in both natures. And if this be proved, if he be the Son of God in both natures only, then he is not the Son of God in the divine nature only; and to prove that he is the Son of God in both natures only, the Scripture so presents him to us, and no otherwise: And as the Scripture presents him to us, so ought we to believe him to be, and no otherwise.*

Before I enter upon the consideration of what the Scriptures say in this important article of our faith, let us hear what Mr. Collier himself saith in his *Body of Divinity*, under this title: "*How this one God subsisteth in three Persons,*" pg. 44.

> *The sum of all is this, that God is one eternal infinite substantial being, distinguished into Father, Son, and Holy Spirit, and in all three, are divine, and distinct relative properties and operations, yet in all no one wills, no one acts without the other (Gen. 1.1, 2, 26; Heb. 1.2; Job 33.4).*

And pg. 43 *"And this truth, i.e. a plurality in one infinite and eternal God, is clearly to be proved from the Old Testament even from Creation."*

It might be supposed by this his brief description of the deity, that Mr. Collier is orthodox in his opinion concerning the divinity of the Son of God, though in many places he be singular in his expressions: And that his design wherein he is singular and different from others, is very charitable, viz. that his supposed absurdity of making two Sons, or the Sonship of Christ not to be the same at first as it was at last, might be avoided.

Yet whosoever thoroughly weighs his whole discourse, cannot but observe that he speaks at least very doubtfully concerning any existence that the Son of God had in the divine nature, before he was made or manifest in flesh.

Additional Word, pg. 11 § 6: *"That this word God-man was made flesh,—Here it seems lieth the block in the way, that he that was a man, was made a man: The resolve is clear from Scripture, he that was God and man in God's eye, was made so in our eye when made or manifested in flesh."*

It were to be wished that Mr. Collier would yet speak more plainly, that if he think aright, a wrong opinion may not be conceived of him, from his seemingly affected obscurity in his expressions. What is the meaning of this, *"He that was God and man in God's eye, was made so in our eye."* Is it that God the Father always saw him as he was from eternity, existing with him in the deity in both natures God-man, or never existing as God the Son till he was made or manifest in the flesh?

Because of this obscurity, and the jealousies justly conceived that Mr. Collier is very corrupt in his opinion concerning the pre-existence of the Son of God in the divine nature before he assumed flesh; let it now be considered whether the Scriptures present the Lord Christ to us as being the Son of God in both natures only, even those places of Scripture (among others) which Mr. Collier by his false glosses would have us to think do so only present him to us.

> Heb. 1.8-9,
> "But unto the Son he saith, thy throne O God is forever and ever, a scepter of righteousness is the scepter of thy Kingdom, thou hast loved righteousness and hated iniquity, therefore God thy God hath anointed thee with the oil of gladness above thy fellows."

Herein we have not only the unction of the Son of God mentioned, but the reason of it: And that is plainly taken from his everlasting divinity, regality, and righteousness. Because he that is the Son of God, is God that made, and upholds, and rules over the world in righteousness, and loveth it, and hateth iniquity, therefore as the only fit person is he anointed by God the Father, his God and our God, to the office of mediatorship, which the whole chapter treats of: And from the dignity of his person as the Son of God, is divine adoration given to him, when as the Son of man, he came first into the world: And from thence also his preeminence, notwithstanding his debasement in the flesh, continues with him above all his fellows.

> Heb. 2.16,
> "He took not on him the nature of angels, but be took on him the seed of Abraham."

If the question be asked (as the Eunuch did Philip in the like case) of whom does the Apostle here speak? The answer is plain from the context of the Son of God. He is the person assuming, reflecting upon the different natures angelical and human, rejecting the former, laying hold of the latter; for here the dignity of the nature of angels, though in itself superior to the human, and more near to the nature of God, as being purely spiritual (and who are in that respect by way of eminency called the Sons of God, Job 38.7), was not chosen: Because the assumption of the human nature, though in itself more inferior, was yet more proper and necessary for their sakes for whom he was the anointed of God as their high priest and savior. Hence is plainly inferred, not only his pre-existence as the Son of God, before his choice and assumption of the seed of Abraham, viz. his taking upon him flesh; but that he was also purely so subsisting in the divine nature, as to stand indifferent as to the assumption of the angelical or human nature into the unity of his person, otherwise than as he was pre-determined by the decree, counsel, and covenant of God, in order to the work to which he was anointed.

> John 16.28,
> "I came forth from the Father, and am come into the world again, I leave the world and go to the Father."

> John 17.5,
> "And now O Father glorify thou me with thine own self, with the glory I had with thee before the world was."

> John 8.42, 58,
> "If God were your Father you would love me; for I proceeded forth, and came from God; neither came I of myself, but he sent me.—Before Abraham was I am."

What words can express more directly the relation of Christ unto God the Father as his Son, considered singly in his divine nature, it was some 1,000 of years after Abraham that we had the knowledge of this mystery by divine revelation, God manifest in flesh, "**the Word was made flesh.**" That was accomplished in the "**fullness of time.**" But from all eternity he was the "**I Am**," the Son of God, and as such came forth from God. And herein also we may note, that he declares (not only his own action and motion, but also his Father's) his mission. It was not only his own undertaking, though he was therein also voluntary. Wherefore he saith, when he cometh into the world, "**Sacrifice and offering thou wouldst not, but a body hast thou prepared me. Then said I, lo I come to do thy will O God.**" In order to the perfect observance of this will of his Father, for the performance whereof he had in time a body prepared, fitted for him which he had not before. The Father sends him and he comes (both are active and spontaneous herein) for the accomplishing of this great work, the reconciliation, redemption and salvation of sinful and lost man.

The Lord Christ did not then first acquire his being or relation unto God the Father as his Son: But being from eternity the brightness of his Father's glory, and express image of his person, after he had by the appointment of his Father, and his own voluntary undertaking, veiled his deity, humbled himself, and taken upon him the form of a servant, and therein performed the work his Father gave him to do, he prays to be restored to the same, not any other, for there could be no greater glory conferred upon him as to his divine nature, than what he had with his Father before the world was.

> John 6.38,
> "I came down out of Heaven, not to do mine own will, but the will of him that sent me."

> Gal. 4.4, 6,
> "When the fullness of time was come God sent out his Son. And because you are sons God hath sent out the Spirit of his Son into your hearts," &c.

In these texts compared with their contexts, you have again a full discovery of him who was by God the Father, anointed to be the savior of the world. His being in the flesh was now manifest to all that conversed with him, it needed no proof, he carried about with him a self-demonstration, that he was "**made of a woman, made under the Law.**" The great thing that the Jews, and all the world were to be fully informed in and convinced of, was, that the person now manifest in the flesh, was the savior, the Christ, the Lord. And for the evidencing of this great and important truth, it was necessary that the Lord Christ should not only speak and do as never man before him spake and did, but also prove his descent, whence he was, and wherefore he came into the world. And in that respect, together with all the testimonies born of him immediately from Heaven by God the Father and the holy angels, we have him frequently asserting his original himself, "**I came down from Heaven.**" Hence it was that the Jews at this season took occasion for their murmuring, John 6.42, "**Is not this Jesus the Son of Joseph, whose father and mother we know, how is it then that he saith, I came down from Heaven.**" In answer to this objection, the Lord Christ tells the Jews, that in order to a true saving knowledge of his person, who and whence he was, it was necessary they should be taught of God; "**Blessed art thou Simon Barjona, for flesh and blood hath not revealed this to thee, but my Father which is in Heaven.**" And that they might know his original, and his immediate and uninterrupted relation to God as his Father, notwithstanding his then present state of Humiliation in the flesh, he tells them from whence he was, who he was, and wherefore he came into the world. The medium he uses to prove his relation to God as his Father, is not his being born of a virgin, Abraham's or David's Seed (though that be also true, and most proper to prove him who is the Son of God to be also that Son of Man, the Messiah that was promised), but he proves it by his descent from Heaven, his seeing of the Father (which no man ever did or could do), his being of God. And because the exceptions to what he affirmed, both by the Jews and his Disciples, were taken from his being in the flesh, therefore to show that the hypostatical union of God and man in him, had not deprived him of his dignity of the Son of God, he speaks of himself under the notion as they apprehended him, of being the Son of Man as he then also was. And asks his Disciples, "**What and if you see the Son of Man ascend up where he was before**," which is further explained John 3.13-14; 12.32; Eph. 4.10. His condescension to take upon him flesh, to become the Son of Man, and in that nature to suffer death upon the Cross, was no deprivation of his divinity, nor derogation from his person, he still asserts, even from thence, his then present being in Heaven. The divine and human nature subsisting in his person, had not removed the deity out of Heaven, but by that intimate conjunction given the humanity from the dignity of his person, a claim to Heaven, and right of Ascension thither. He did not therefore descend, that he might always remain upon earth, but that after he had finished his Father's work which he was to do in the flesh, he might carry the human nature with him into Heaven, whither he was to ascend again. So that since his uniting of the human to the divine nature in his own person, whether he was spoken of as the Son of God according to his divinity, or as the Son of David according to his humanity, under which notion soever he was spoken of, either as the Son of God, or the Son of Man, he being in both natures but one entire person, was still truly said to be in Heaven; not that it was, or could ever be supposed that his claim to Heaven, and his being there, did arise from his being the Son of Man, but as he himself asserts from his coming down from thence, his coming, and being sent from his Father, and yet remaining always with his Father, "**He and his Father being one.**" He that descended is the same also that ascended; there neither was, nor could there be admitted any change of the person. It is also observable that, Gal. 4.6, the same word is used for the sending forth of the Spirit of his Son by God the Father, into the hearts of his adopted sons, that is used for the sending forth of his Son into the world. This is no slender evidence of the eternity and divinity of Christ, that he hath the same relation to the Holy Spirit with the

Father (1 Pet. 1.11). It was the Spirit of Christ that was in the Prophets of old, that long before his Incarnation did foretell thereof, and of his sufferings, and the Glory that should follow: David himself said by his Spirit, "**The Lord said unto my Lord, sit thou at my right hand till I make thine enemies thy footstool**," as to his divinity he is the root of David, who according to his humanity was his offspring (Rev. 22.16).

The vision of Isaiah ch. 6 was true, and the voice of the angels a real voice, who cried as to the time then present, "**holy, holy, holy is the Lord of Hosts, the whole Earth is full of his glory**." And if the application of this vision of the Prophet, and voice of the angels by the Evangelist (John 12.41) be also true, what more clear evidence can be given of the Lord Christ's subsisting in the Divine nature, before his descension from Heaven and assumption of the human nature.

> "**Thou Lord in the beginning hast laid the foundation of the Earth, and the Heavens are the work of thine hands; they shall perish, but thou remainest, they shall wax old as doth a garment, and as a vesture thou shalt fold them up; and they shall be changed, but thou art the same, and thy years shall not fail.**"

From these and many other the like texts, is the divinity of the Lord Christ fully asserted, and by the writings of the Apostles, directed by the Holy Spirit, since his Incarnation applied to him. By whom we are given to understand, that the Prophets aforetime spoke of our Lord Christ, and thereby is made known to us the dignity of his person, as the Alpha and Omega. But I would have Mr. Collier ingeniously consider, whether he or any other man, without this future revelation and explication, could have gathered any such doctrine as the manhood coexisting with the Godhead in the person of Christ from all eternity; or that he who in the beginning laid the foundations of the Earth, and made the Heavens, was when he did this work man as well as God; or that since this revelation and application of these sayings to the person of Christ, can say any otherwise than that these titles and operations are referred to the Son of God as he subsisted in his divine nature with the Father. And if this be so, let Mr. Collier be convinced and acknowledge, that the Scriptures do sometimes (and that frequently) speak of the Son of God as in the divine nature only, and not always as he was in both natures God and man.

CHAPTER II

Of Election

I shall for the better order sake pass over his second chapter at present and consider in the next place what he proposeth in his third, of Election.

Only this I desire the reader to take notice of once for all, that I intend not to make Mr. Collier's discourse an occasion of going over the heads of the controversy betwixt us and the Arminians, in a full stating and handling of those points: It hath been sufficiently done by others both formerly and of late; but my present design is only to remove those stumbling-blocks, that he in this book hath endeavored to cast before weak Christians. Thus he begins, pg. 18:

> *"Of this I have spoken something too in my Confession of Faith, or Body of Divinity; but in this I shall speak a little more full and plain."*

I will not undertake to justify all he hath said about Election in his *Body of Divinity*; but I must say, that in this he is gone farther out of the way of truth, and instead of speaking more full and plain to the business, he involves himself in many absurdities and gross errors which before he kept off from. He proceeds to explain the term:

> "Election, or to elect or choose, from ἐκλεκτός, or ἐκλογή,[1] in Scripture ordinarily imports to choose, or to be chosen."

What Mr. Collier designs in getting these Greek words into his book, I know not: One that understands not the Greek can tell him, that to "elect" or "choose," ordinarily imports to choose. But I confess he must have more learning than I, that can readily conceive how, to elect or choose, should import "to be chosen," which Mr. Collier adds: Election indeed is sometimes put to signify "persons chosen;" the abstract being put for the concrete.

He proceeds to his division of Election; unto which I shall oppose a brief account thereof from the Scripture, and so free the term from ambiguity, that we may proceed without interruption.

Election as it is attributed to God may be variously considered:

1. There is frequent mention in Scripture of Election unto some function or office either ecclesiastical or political.

2. There is an Election unto a participation of some peculiar benefits and favors from God; and this may be distinguished into that which is,

    1. General, in which sense a person or nation is said to be chosen of God, when they partake of such an adoption as that they are brought into some covenant with God, and are reputed his people: so the Israelites, were an elect nation.

---

[1] *"Chosen out, selected; choosing out, selecting, choice."*

2. Special; and that is God's choosing unto eternal life, and it is either of angels, or men: And it is this Election, and the concernment of men therein, that we are to consider; and as Mr. Polhil well observes (pg. 24, of the Div. Will²), this is variously expressed in the Scripture: It is called πρόθεσις³ (Rom. 8.28) because it is God's *purpose*: πρόθεσις καί χάρις⁴ (2 Tim. 1.9) because his gracious purpose: ἐκλογη,⁵ (Rom. 11.6) because he separates or singles out some to mercy in a way of choice: πρόγνωσις⁶ (1 Pet. 1.2) because he knows them as his own in a way of singular love: προορισμός⁷ (Rom. 8.29-30) because he infallibly predestinates them to grace and glory: and εὐδοκία τοῦ θελήματος⁸ (Eph. 1.5) because all is out of the pure self-motion of his own good will. This Election of God then is,

"God willing or decreeing to glorify his grace in the salvation of a certain number of the posterity of fallen man, through sanctification of the Spirit, and belief of the truth."

And other Election unto eternal life, the Scripture knoweth not.

So then what Mr. Collier discourseth, pg. 19, concerning a general election in the Gospel, hath no foundation but in the ambiguity of the term, which I have removed: And indeed in the New Testament there is no countenance given to the using of the term in

---

² Edward Polhill, *The Divine Will Considered in its Eternal Decrees, and Holy Execution of them* (London: Henry Eversden, 1673), 24. The sentence beginning with "It is called" is a quotation from Polhill.
³ *"Deliberate purpose."*
⁴ *"Deliberate purpose and grace."*
⁵ *"Choosing out, selecting, choice."*
⁶ *"Foreknowledge."*
⁷ *"Foredetermination."*
⁸ *"Good-pleasure* or *favour of his will."*

that sense as he doth: when whole churches are said to be elect; it is rather because in the judgment of charity each member in a Gospel church is so to be esteemed, than for the reason which he supposeth. That which he drops in that Section concerning falling from grace, shall be examined afterwards.

He proceeds, pg. 20, to discourse of Special Election, which he makes twofold.

The first is of these who are chosen in Christ before the foundation of the world, unto the obtaining of grace and glory: A brief account of which I have already given. The reason he gives for this is, *"That the undertaking of Christ might be assured not to be in vain on the most special account,"* &c.

He acknowledgeth then, that if there had not been a certain number given to Christ by the Father, who by effectual grace should be brought to believe in him, his undertaking might have been in vain: But this must not be: Very true: But then if the whole of his undertaking must not be left at uncertainty, why should any part of it be so? How Mr. Collier will reconcile this with his other notions I know not. He goes on,

> *"The second sort of special Election in the Gospel is of all that do believe and obey the Gospel in truth, persevering therein to the end."*

Afterwards he accounts these distinct from the special Elect; but for the present he makes this one branch of special Election: I shall allow him to alter his terms as he pleaseth, if he find them unfit, and consider his present notion, which is built upon this supposition, that many may and shall believe and obey the Gospel, and persevere therein to the end, that receive no special grace from God in the pursuit of his electing love, to enable them thereunto, or preserve them therein (which notion shall be examined in its proper place). And these are Elected on the foresight of their faith and obedience and perseverance therein. And here we might reasonably expect, that

Thomas Collier in his *Additional Word*, should have confuted the arguments urged against such an Election by Thomas Collier in his *Body of Divinity* pg. 444-446. But this he silently passeth over; and this sudden change is the more to be taken notice of, because he tells us in his preface to that book, that "*They are not the notions of sudden conception, but the fruit and birth of many years travel; that he there presents us with: And that he would have all his doctrine to be compared with that book; and either reconciled therewith or rejected.*" I know some will be ready to say,

Inconstans levitas, levis inconstantia vulgi!
Nunc vult, nunc non vult, & nunc neq; vult, neq; non vult!⁹

But I shall rather mind that seasonable exhortation of the Apostle, Eph. 4.14 and Heb. 12.9 and so address myself to consider what proof of this notion he offers to us.

"*Election*," saith he, "*under this consideration is declared in these and the like Scriptures, John 6.40; 3.16; 8.31; Rom. 2.7; Heb. 5.9; Col. 1.21, 23; Rev. 22.14.*" All these Scriptures hold forth no more but the inseparable connection (as of the means with the end) of faith and obedience persevered in, with eternal life and salvation; not a tittle of the Election of any on the foresight of these. "**He that holdeth out to the end shall be saved,**" which all the Elect shall do, being kept by the power of God through faith unto salvation; but this grace, as well as future glory, floweth to them from the eternal spring of electing love.

Yea Mr. Collier himself can tell us at another time, that "*Faith is nowhere stated in the Scriptures as the condition of Election; neither in reason can it be so, if we consider what persons are Elected to, and that is to believe and obey the Gospel, to be holy here and happy hereafter, 1 Pet. 1.2.*" *Body of Divinity* pg. 445.

---

[9] A literal translation might be: "*Unstable/unsteady changeableness, the changeable unsteadiness of the crowd! Now he wishes, now he does not wish, and now he cannot, he wishes, he cannot, he does not wish!*" The general idea is to highlight the instability of some people.

And if Mr. Collier will consult those that have written on this controversy, he may find other arguments urged against this error also, but perhaps his own may have the greatest influence on him. I shall therefore leave that with him, and attend him in his farther offer of proof of the contrary opinion now. Thus he proceeds, pg. 21,

> *"We may not so understand particular and special Election, as to derogate from the universal grace and love of God to all men; nor from the truth of the Law of Grace, which calleth upon all, and encourageth all, and promiseth life to all that do believe and obey the Gospel," &c.*

What Mr. Collier means by the universal grace and love of God to all men he doth not here explain: But by the tenor of his discourse in other places in his book, his sense appears to be, that God intended the redemption and salvation of all men in the death of his Son, and hath recovered them all out of their fallen state, and put them into a capacity of obtaining Heaven, without his special grace. And it is true, that the doctrine of Election as revealed in the Scriptures, doth overthrow this fiction; but must it therefore be rejected, because it will not comport with his errors? And whereas he supposeth that the Decree of God concerning the salvation of the Elect opposeth his revealed will, and gracious invitations unto sinners in the Gospel; this must be imputed to his ignorance of these things: He tells us not wherein he supposeth the opposition doth lie, and whatever he thinks, their harmony is sweet and full. There is a sufficiency in Christ to save the whole world if they did believe on him, and there is a sure promise of salvation to every believer: And it is the will of God that salvation by Christ should be rendered unto all where the Gospel comes on the terms mentioned therein; but the wickedness, of man's heart, and his natural enmity to God being such, as would render all this fruitless if he were left to himself; the most high did from everlasting Decree (that which in time he effects), by his powerful grace to draw a remnant unto Christ, that they may obtain salvation by him, and to leave the rest to perish in their obstinacy. Where then is our making null the revealed will of God by his Decree, that Mr. Collier talks of? He adds, "*The Lord himself makes this distinction, with suitable promises alike to both,*" i.e. "*He allows a latitude beyond the first and special Election, or gift to his Son, with promise of life on the universal account of grace,*" *John 6.37*, which text he miserably wrests in his following lines; unto the whole my answer is briefly this:

The Decree of God is one thing, his command another; it is the latter that constitutes our duty, not the former. It doth not therefore follow, that because many are called, and commanded to believe, and life is tendered to them on Gospel-terms; therefore many are chosen besides the special Elect. But to the text: "**All that the Father giveth me shall come to me, and him that cometh unto me I will in no wise cast out.**" In the context Christ declares,

1. That there was a certain number given to him by the Father; which Mr. Collier owns to be the special Elect.

2. That concerning these the will of God was, that they should be brought to inherit eternal life by faith in Christ, v. 40.

3. That although the natural pravity of men is such, that no man without special grace can come to Christ, v. 44. Yet these should by the drawings of the Father be brought to him, "**All that the Father hath given me, shall come to me.**"

4. That these coming should in no wise be rejected by him; and the reason thereof he renders, v. 38, 39. It is evident therefore the same persons are spoken of in the end, that are intended in the beginning of v. 37, and Mr. Collier's supposition of the contrary is without ground; and his reason for it ridiculous; "*It cannot be supposed,*" saith he, "*that him that cometh, &c. is a promise to the first gift, for they shall come, that is,*"

> *All the Elect shall believe in Christ; ergo, there is no promise made of their salvation by him. Apage nugas!*[10]

That which he discourseth concerning the Book of Life, pg. 22, if his notion of it were granted, makes nothing for him, unless he suppose that the revealed will of God, that declares and determines our duty, what we ought to do; and the Decree of God, or what himself will do; to be all one. However we will consider what he saith, viz. That "*Rev. 3.5 & 2.12, 15 & 22.19 must be understood to speak of the Gospel Book of Life, in which all believers are written, and not the first Book of Life in which the special Elect are written.*"

I answer,

1. The special Elect and true believers are terms convertible, where the one are written, the other are written: And it is Mr. Collier's great error to suppose the number of the one to exceed the other: As many as are ordained to eternal life believe, so the Election obtain, and the rest are blinded, Acts 13.48; Rom. 11.7.

2. A book is attributed to God in Scripture, not properly, but by a figure called Anthropopatheia; the metaphor being taken from wise men, who are wont diligently to set down in a book those notable things that they would keep in mind, and signifieth his providence with respect to, and most exact knowledge of all things, and in the Scriptures cited by Mr. Collier it signifies God's special knowledge of his saved ones, concerning which the Apostle speaks, 2 Tim. 2.19, which is as a certain catalogue of those whom God hath chosen unto eternal life by faith in Christ: But Mr. Collier saith, they must

---

[10] "*Away with your jesting!*"

be otherwise understood: His saying they must is no proof; and his reasons are too weak to inforce it. His first is, "*because out of the Book of Life here mentioned many may be blotted.*" I answer, the expression is figurative, and is to be interpreted according to the scope of the place; as God is said to blot out sin, when he doth not impute it, so to blot out the name of one out of the Book of Life, that he doth not reckon among his saved ones, which he will make manifest in the Day of Judgment, when all the world shall know that he had no part therein; thus the affirmative being put for the contrary negative; the sense is briefly this, God shall take away his part out of the Book of Life, Rev. 22.19. i.e. He shall have no part at all in it, and so likewise *e contra*,[11] ch. 3, v. 5, "**I will not blot out his name out of the Book of Life,**" i.e. I will reckon him amongst my own sheep, and it shall appear by my confessing him before my Father, &c.

His second reason is, "*Because this Book is one of those by which men shall be judged*," Rev. 20.12, 15.

In the text this book is mentioned distinct from those by which men shall be judged; and the opening of it in that day signifies the glorious discovery that shall then be made of the Lord, his having ordered all things in his holy and righteous government of the world, so as to fulfill his own Decree, and that all his saved ones are alone beholding to free grace dispensed according to the purpose that God purposed in himself before the foundation of the world; for in the issue (when men have talked their pleasure of their own ability) it so comes to pass, that whatsoever was not written in the Book of Life, was cast into the Lake of Fire, not simply because they were not written there, but because they being left to the way of their own heart, did willfully persist in their rebellion against God, for which they must then suffer the vengeance of eternal fire.

---

[11] "*From the opposite.*"

"*Election,*" he saith, "*is no ground to discourage any from believing;*" who saith it is? That crimination hath been abundantly answered by others without the help of his Scriptureless notion.

The tenders of life in the Gospel are full of grace, the command to believe, equal and rational; and the promise of life to the believer sure and steadfast: Election is a secret and hidden thing, as to the concernment of particular persons in it, which belongeth unto God, and as none can know their Election of God before faith, so is it no way necessary that they should do so in order to believing: For revealed things belong unto us and our children, and we are bound to attend to them in that same order in which God hath revealed them: Now in the Gospel is the salvation of God revealed to lost sinners, and they, simply considered as such, commanded to accept of it upon the terms proposed to them; none are called to believe under the formal consideration of Elect persons; but as weary and heavy laden sinners; undone thirsty sinners; in which terms every one sensible of his condition by nature, finds himself presently, and equally with others concerned. Now, that God hath purposed to make this call effectual unto some, and, these upon believing, through the doctrine of Election, have a prospect into the heart of God towards them, and his everlasting purpose of grace concerning them, and find their spiritual and glorious joy increased, by a knowledge that their names are written in Heaven; being rightly weighed may on divers accounts encourage, but on no account can discourage the faith of any.

We come now to his last section in this chapter, which is worse than all that goes before; yet here he gives us but a taste of what he intends more largely to pursue afterwards. Thus, he writes pg. 23:

> "*The Scripture seems to import that many, yea very many (compared with the first elect and espoused relation) shall obtain some great privilege, though below that of Election, and espoused relation to Jesus Christ.*"

That which he was to prove is, that besides those that are chosen to the obtaining of grace and glory, there are others chosen to be heirs of glory on foresight of their faith, &c. so that they obtain Election thereby. To make this good, he tells us of very many that shall obtain some great privilege, though below that of Election. Such impertinencies are his writings full of, but we will take his meaning to be, that they he now speaks of shall obtain the second Election, but not the first; which is a great privilege, but below that of espoused relation to Christ. But then is he at variance with himself again; for thus he writes a little before, pg. 16, "*Whoever among the sons and daughters of men, do sincerely believe and obey the Gospel, shall have the special relation to God and Christ therein, and the special benefit and salvation thereof.*" And this he supposeth many do besides the special elect; and in this very chapter he tells us, that faith and obedience with perseverance therein, renders persons the objects of this Election; and certainly the Scriptures know no other espoused relation to Christ, but what we have by faith; neither are there greater promises in the book of God, than those that are made to persons persevering in faith and obedience; "**They shall inherit all things**" (Rev. 21.7). But Mr. Collier supposeth that these believe, and persevere with less help from God than the special Elect have. Be it so, there is no reason that this should lessen their glory; why therefore Mr. Collier sets these beneath the special Elect, I know not. But indeed these are saints of his own making, and therefore he may prefer, or postpone them as he pleaseth. The Scripture speaks of no true believers, but the Elect that are enabled to believe by special grace.

He proceeds to his proof; "*Else,*" saith he, "*what means that Psalm 45.14, 'The virgins her companions that follow her shall be brought unto thee,' i.e. to Christ, where the only one spouse is distinct from the virgins her companions.*" Mr. Collier it seems is confident this can have no other meaning but what favors his notion. But here it were easy for me to fill up divers sheets in transcribing the commentaries of many learned men on this text, of which not one gives countenance to his opinion; but that suits not with my present design: Briefly therefore I reply,

In this Psalm, and in Solomon's Song (from whence he takes his next testimony), the Holy Ghost doth set forth things spiritual and heavenly by types, and metaphors, taken from things terrene, and usages among men; which necessarily fall short of the complete expression of the glory of the things of God's Kingdom; and therefore as there is somewhat of similitude, so is there also of dissimilitude betwixt the things compared, and the parallel must not be run farther than the scope of the texts themselves, and warranty of other plain Scriptures will allow: Hence it is also that divers metaphors are used to express the same thing, of which some do adumbrate it under this respect, and some under that. Now in this Scripture the manifest design of the Psalmist is to set forth the majesty and grace of Christ's Kingdom, as he is the head and husband of his people, together with the glorious privileges of the Church his spouse, in her marriage relation to him: And therefore in his description of the Church, in that state and honor unto which Christ hath advanced her, she is compared to a queen richly adorned, and attended (as with her ladies of honor) by the virgins her companions; because so it useth to be with queens when brought in state unto their lord and husband. And if we strain the metaphor (or type) no farther, we have a good sense of the words, and that which suits the design of the text. Although I am inclined to think, that the same Church, and spouse of Christ is in various respects shadowed, by either term, both of "**queen**," and of "**the virgins her companions:**" As she is represented by the queen, respect is had to the then flourishing state of the Jewish church; as by the virgins her companions, that should also be brought to Christ, the bringing in of the Gentiles, and their gathering into divers particular congregations is respected, which in the fullness of time should be, though then they were as a little sister that had no breasts. More might be added, but this sufficeth to show that he hath failed of his purpose in the citation of this text. He proceeds,

> *And that Song 9.6 [he means the 6.8-9] where are multitudes, besides the espoused relation, of queens [but*

certainly if they be queens indeed, they are espoused to him whose queens they are], concubines and virgins, blessing and praising the holy and happy estate of the undefiled spouse; called, 5.8, the 'daughters of Jerusalem:' So that there may be many friends and followers, that may come short of the espoused relation, and yet have a part at that day.

As to Cant. 6.8, 9, Here seems to be two things of a different nature, one referring to the ways of the kings of the Earth, and another referring to Jesus Christ; the kings of the Earth use to have many queens and concubines, many single persons for their pleasure and recreation, and Solomon himself was greatly presumptuous in this kind; but speaking of Christ's disposition, he is not like the world, but saith, "**My love, my dove is but one, and she is the only one of her mother, and the choice one of her that bear her**:" as there is but one Christ, so in matter of salvation there is but one Church. And therefore I see not at present any just exception against the account that Mr. Ainsworth gives of it in his annotations, which is to this purpose,[12]

"**There are sixty**," or "**be there sixty queens**," i.e. Though there were sixty, &c. yet one is my dove, or there is but one my dove, so this one only is opposed to the many queens, concubines, &c. beforementioned: Here the spouse of Christ, which is but one (as there is but one body, and one spirit, one hope, one Lord, one Faith even as we are called in one hope of our calling, Eph. 4.4-5) is preferred before the multitude of other, which in their own, and the world's esteem are queens, ladies, &c. Rev. 18.7; Isa. 47.7—"**and they praised her.**" The spouse is counted happy for the great blessings of God upon her, as it is said of Israel, Deut. 26.19, that God had made them high above all nations which he had made, in praise and in name, and in honor; so the people magnified Christians, Acts 5.13.

---

[12] Henry Ainsworth, *Annotations upon the Five Books of Moses, the Book of Psalmes, and the Song of Songs, or Canticles* (London: John Bellamie, 1627), 45. Pagination begins anew with each Bible book. Ainsworth (1569-1622) led a church in exile in the Netherlands. He was a noted Hebraist and expositor. See the entry in the *Oxford Dictionary of National Biography*.

By the daughters of Jerusalem in this book we may understand those that under some common or preparatory work of the Spirit, have some respect to Christ and his Church, though they are not perfectly brought over to him, or fully instructed in his way, but inquiring after it (see 5.8-9 & 6.1). Now in such, either the Lord carries on this work unto a thorough conversion, and so the uniting of the soul unto himself by faith, and then are they among his espoused and saved ones, or else they sin away their convictions, and return again with the sow that was washed to wallowing in the mire, and the latter end of such is worse than theirs who never made a profession.

Hitherto then Mr. Collier can find out no persons in the Scripture to fill up his imagined middle room betwixt Heaven and Hell. If persons belong not to that number which make up the Bride the Lamb's wife, the new Jerusalem (notwithstanding his idle talking) there will be no other place found for them in the day of Christ, but amongst those mentioned Rev. 21.8 & 22.14-15. He adds,

> *"And that Matt. 25.1-12 seems to suit with those Scriptures; though the Lord and bridegroom will say to the foolish virgins, I know you not; that may be; in the espoused relation to go into the wedding he knew them not, but as virgins that had been his spouse's companions."*

Certainly Mr. Collier esteems himself able ἀκινητά κινεῖν[13] to overturn things immoveable by a blast of his corrupt doctrine, or else he had never had the confidence to produce this text for the proof of what he brings it for; viz. That many (of which number he reckons these foolish virgins) shall be elected for their faith and obedience, and obtain some great privilege in the day of Christ. Let us therefore consider the character of the persons that he supposeth shall be thus dignified: All indeed that are mentioned in the parable were virgins,

---

[13] *"To move the immoveable."*

viz. in profession; the foolish as well as the wise pretended to purity, and were outwardly conformable to the laws of Christ; but for all this five were foolish, i.e. sinners, such as never in truth knew the things that did belong to their peace; and these had no oil in their vessels, i.e. no true grace in their hearts; they were hypocrites in the midst of their profession; and when Christ came they were found unready, i.e. without a wedding garment of faith and holiness (and this account he gives of them himself in effect in his *Body of Divinity* pg. 135 & 136), and the Lord protests, that he knows them not; but he knows all that are his; they belong not therefore unto Christ, but to the god of this world; they were in heart his vassals; though with their lips they pretended kindness to Christ: And yet this man endeavors to persuade such that they shall have peace; and for all this hypocrisy, because they kept company with others that were sincere, though they were painted sepulchers all the while; they shall have a place in the Kingdom of Glory, though not full out so excellent as that which the special Elect obtain! If this doctrine be according to godliness, I know nothing that deserves to be esteemed contrary thereto. But let not men trust in this refuge of lies, nor cheat their souls with vain hopes, because of the smooth things that Mr. Collier doth prophecy unto them. What in truth will be the condition and state of such as these in the day of Christ, you have graphically described in these texts of Scripture: Matt. 22.12-13 & 13.40-41 compared with 24.51, and this very text compared with 7.21-23 and Prov. 1.28.

As for the other texts cited by him, viz. Matt. 10.41-42 and Matt. 20.16, &c. I cannot devise which way he thinks to put the first of them upon the wrack, so as to make it speak to his mind. That which it teacheth us is, that they which love the members of Christ, and desire the furtherance of his work, do give evidence of their own being in him, and relation to him, and therefore shall be glorified with his servants. This gives no countenance to his notion. In the other, viz.

Matt. 20.16 with Mar. 10.31.[14] If the scope of the parable be attended, the sense will appear to be this, "**Many that are first**," viz. in appearance, as to the earliness of their profession, and their outward forwardness and seeming earliness therein, "**shall be last**," i.e. shall at the last be found castaways, empty of good, and left behind unto destruction; "**and the last**," i.e. many that a while, and to man's eye seemed last, it being either long ere they were professors, which was Paul's case; or for a while very timorous and close, which was the case of Joseph of Arimathea,—"**shall be first**," i.e. shall at the last be found real and precious, and accordingly received and accepted in Christ.

"**For many are called**," viz. not only having had the Gospel preached to them, but being also thereby brought outwardly into the visible Church: "**But few chosen**," i.e. few of the aforesaid many, be God's choice ones taken to himself in everlasting mercy, according to his eternal purpose of saving them. See Matt. 22.14. *Hæc ex notis manuscriptis docti cujusdam simul ac pii jam ἐν μακαρίταις excerpta sunt.*[15]

Mr. Collier proceeds, "*Else what meaneth that of the first fruits to God and to the Lamb, Rev. 14.14, if it do not intend the special saved ones in the Election, and the multitudes that may obtain besides according to the metaphor, as the harvest to the first fruits.*" I answer this text, with James 1.18, hath a meaning very different from what Mr. Collier supposeth: The whole number of Elect regenerate ones are set apart for God as his peculiar people and portion; even as in the time of the Law, the first-fruits were set apart for God, and sanctified unto him: So then as the first-fruits are but an handful to the harvest, so are the saved ones but a remnant, when compared with the multitudes of the world that perish in their sins. "**For wide is the Gate, and broad is the way that leadeth to destruction, and many there be which go in thereat: Because strait is the gate, and narrow is the way which**

---

[14] The original text has a typographical error here, reading "*Mar. 20.31.*" Collier cited Mark 10.31, the parallel to Matthew 20.16.

[15] "*These examples of a certain and at the same time righteous teaching have been chosen from well-known passages by the blessed.*" "*Blessed*" presumably refers to earlier believing authors.

leadeth unto life, and few there be that find it. Beware of false prophets" (Matt. 7.13-15). But, saith he,

> *"It would be beneath the spirit and charity of the Gospel, to allow no salvation (during the Old Covenant) to any in the world besides the elect Church of the Jews, and contrary to the Scripture, Acts 10.34-35."*

In what sense the nation of the Israelites was chosen of God, I showed before: That all are not Israel (elect of God to eternal life) that are of Israel (according to the flesh), is certain; and I grant also, that in the time Mr. Collier speaks of God had his remnant (though we have reason to think not many) in other nations, unto whom he did by means ordinary or extraordinary manifest himself; and these did fear God, and work righteousness by which their Election of God was manifested: But that these did not belong to the number of the special Elect, nor were of that Church which is Christ's Spouse, is utterly untrue, neither doth he attempt to prove it. He saith moreover,

> *"—Or to allow no salvation now under the Gospel, to any among the Gentiles that have not heard of Christ; and contrary to the Scripture, Rom. 2.14-16."*

Mr. Collier's notion about this matter, we shall meet with again and examine afterwards: At the present I must tell him, that without the Spirit and grace of Christ, which may not be separate from the knowledge of him, and faith in his name; all that persons can do, is from a principle of self-love to yield some obedience to the Law of God externally, and so live honestly among men: **But by the deeds of the Law shall no flesh be justified in God's sight; for by the Law is the knowledge of sin**, Rom. 3.21, and that the law of nature, where the written Law is wanting, will so far supply the place thereof, as to convince of sin, and leave the sinner inexcusable in his disobedience, is the design of the Apostle to evince, Rom. 2.14, "**When the Gentiles** which have not the Law," (viz. written) "**do by nature**" (i.e. by a knowledge and conscience which God causeth to remain in man's nature, though corrupt), "**do** τά τοῦ νόμου[16] **the offices of the law**," viz. condemning evil and in their consciences approving good, not so as to love good and hate evil, but this they did sufficiently unto full inexcusableness; "**These having not the Law, are a law unto themselves**," &c.

So Mr. Collier closeth this chapter without proof of his opinion.

---

[16] *"The things of the law"* or more specifically as Coxe renders the phrase, *"the offices of the law."*

CHAPTER III

Of the Extent of Christ's Death

I return now to his second chapter, where he discourseth of the extent of the design of God in the death of his Son, wherein he is so extremely confused, contradictious to himself, Scripture, and reason, that I fear the censure of my reader for abusing him, with the repetition of Mr. Collier's absurdities, that can justly plead for no answer; and also for employing my own precious time to no better purposes; but that which first engaged me in this task must be my plea for proceeding in my reply to this and the remaining part of his book.

In the beginning of this chapter, pg. 13, after he hath minded us of differing apprehensions among men concerning the end of Christ's death, that he may be sure to outstrip all, he tells us:

> "That Christ died for the world, that is the universe, the Heavens and Earth all things therein, the whole six days Creation that fell with man for the sin of man," &c.

Certainly whatsoever the Scripture holdeth forth concerning the curse brought upon the Creation by the sin of man, and the future deliverance of the creature from the vanity it now groans under, it cannot but found very harsh to Christian ears, to hear, that their savior died for the universe, yea for all things in Heaven or Earth, for every silly bird that flies in the air, yea and every creature known in nature, even the vilest, most perishing and contemptible thing: Yea, how ridiculous might this notion be rendered; but I fear God, and therefore dare not dally with those things wherein the dying of my precious Lord must be mentioned. This woeful mistake he is cast upon by the ambiguity of the word "**world**," which he supposeth must always intend the universe, but the absurdity of that hypothesis abundantly appears if we look into divers texts where the word is used, and can in no wise bear that sense: Mr. Collier doth also assert universal redemption in the Arminian sense in the next section: Because this word and the term "**all**" is sometimes used in Scripture where redemption by Christ is treated of: And so do others more sober than he: For an answer therefore unto his abuse of divers texts (even all that are with any color pleaded by him) and fully to deliver the weak from his snares; as also that my reader may not complain of the utter loss of his time; I will briefly give an account of those two terms from the reverend Dr. Owen his Treatise of Redemption; which I the rather insert, because that excellent treatise is now grown scarce, and in the hands of few of those for whose benefit these lines are especially designed. Thus he writes:

> Two words there are that are mightily stuck upon or stumbled at: First, the 'world.' Secondly, 'all.' The particular places wherein they are, and from which the arguments of our adversaries are urged, we shall afterwards consider, and for the present only show that the words themselves according to the Scripture use, do not necessarily hold out any collective universality of those, concerning whom they are affirmed: But being

words of various significations, must be interpreted according to the scope of the place where they are used, and the subject matter of which the Scripture treateth in those places.

First then for the word 'world,' which in the New Testament is called κόσμος (for there is another word sometimes translated 'world,' viz. αἰών that belongs not to this matter, noting rather the duration of time, than the thing in that space continuing) he that doth not acknowledge it to be πολίσημον[1] (i.e. a word of various significations) need say no more to manifest this unacquaintedness in the book of God: I shall briefly give you so many various significations of it, as shall make it apparent, that from the bare usage of a word, so exceedingly equivocal, no argument can be taken, until it be distinguished, and the meaning thereof in that particular place evinced, from whence the argument is taken.[2]

I shall pass over the scheme inserted by the Learned Author, because it is contained in what followeth, which is more accommodate to mean capacities. He proceeds,

The word 'world' in the Scripture is in general taken four ways. First, *pro mundo continente*,[3] and that first generally ὁλῶς[4] for the whole fabric of Heaven and Earth, with all

---

[1] "*Of many meanings.*" The English term "polysemous" is derived from this Greek term.
[2] John Owen, *Salus Electorum, Sanguis Jesu, or, The Death of Death in the Death of Christ* (London: Philemon Stephens, 1648), 182; William Goold, ed. *The Works of John Owen* (Edinburgh: The Banner of Truth, 1978 reprint), X:303. The second lengthy quotation is from the same work, pages 183-187 and in the reprint X:304-09. Owen, followed by Coxe, says "the word *World* in the Scripture is in general taken four ways" and then provides five examples! The Banner of Truth edition alters "*four*" to "*five.*"
[3] "*For the world contained,*" i.e. as he notes, with reference to the cosmos. Notice that Owen's second point begins with this phrase, rendered in English, but with a more limited referent.
[4] "*Wholly.*"

things in them contained, which in the beginning were created of God so, Job 34.13; Acts 17.24; Eph 1.4, and in very many other places. Secondly distinctly; first for the Heavens and all things belonging to them distinguished from the Earth, Psalm 90.2. Secondly the habitable earth, and this very frequently, as Psalm 24.1; 98.7.

Secondly, for the world contained, especially men in the world, and that either first universally for all and every one, Rom. 3.6, 19; 5.12. Secondly indefinitely, for men without restriction or enlargement, John 7.4; Isa. 13.11. Thirdly exegetically, for 'many,' which is the most usual acceptation of the word, Matt. 18.7; John 4.42; 12.19; 16.1; 17.21; 1 Cor. 4.9; Rev. 13.3. Fourthly comparatively, for a great part of the world, Rom. 1.8; 10.18; Matt. 24.14; 26.13. Fifthly restrictively, for the inhabitants of the Roman Empire, Luke 2.1. Sixthly, for men distinguished from their several qualifications; as first for the good; God's people either in designation or possession, Psalm 22.27; John 3.16; 6.33,[5] 51; Rom. 4.13; 11.12, 15; 2 Cor. 5.19; Col. 1.6; 1 John 2.2. Secondly, for the evil, wicked, and rejected men of the world, John 7.7; 14.17, 22; 15.19; 17.25; 1 Cor. 6.2; 11.32; Heb. 9.11; 11.38; 2 Pet. 2.5; 1 John 5.19; Rev. 13.3.

Thirdly, for the world corrupted, or that universal corruption that is in all things in it, as Gal. 1.4; 4.1, 4; 6.14; Eph. 2.2; James 1.27; 4.4; 1 John 2.15-17; 1 Cor. 7.31, 33; Col. 2.8; 2 Tim. 4.10; Rom. 12.2; 1 Cor. 1.20-21; 3.18-19.

Fourthly, for a terrene worldly estate or condition of men or things, Psalm 73.12; Luke 16.8; John 18.36; 1 John 4.5, and very many other places.

---

[5] Originally 6:36, corrected to 6:33.

Fifthly, for the world accursed, as under the power of Satan, John 7.7; 14.30; 16.11, 33; 1 Cor. 2.12; 2 Cor. 4.4; Eph. 6.12; and divers other significations hath this word in holy writ, which are needless to recount; these I have rehearsed to show the vanity of that clamor, wherewith some men fill their mouths, and frighten unstable souls, with the Scripture mentioning 'world' so often in the business of redemption; as though some strength might be taken thence for the upholding of the general ransom. *Parvas habet spes Troja, si tales habet.*[6] If their greatest strength be but sophistical craft, taken from the ambiguity of an equivocal word, their whole endeavor is like to prove fruitless. Now as I have declared that it hath divers other acceptations in the Scripture, so when I come to a consideration of their objections that use the word for this purpose; I hope by God's assistance to show, that in no one place wherein it is used in this business of redemption, that it is or can be taken for all and every man in the world, as indeed it is in very few places besides: So that as concerning this word our way will be clear, if to what hath been said ye add these observations.

First, that as in other words, so in this, there is in the Scripture usually an ἀνάκλασις[7] whereby the same word is ingeminated in a different sense and acceptation: So Matt. 8.22, 'Let the dead bury their dead:' 'Dead' in the first place denoting them that are spiritually dead in sin; in the next, those that are naturally dead by a dissolution of soul and body: So John 1.11. 'He came εἰς τὰ ἴδια to his

---

[6] Literally "*Troy has little hope, if she has [but] such as [these],*' an adaptation of a line from Seneca's *Troiades* (Trojan Women) line 742, where Andromache says '*nullas habet spes Troia, si tales habet*' – '*Troy has no hopes if she has but such as these.*' Owen's point seems to be that those teaching this falsehood have little hope of convincing people if they base their argument on (i.e. put their hope in) such minor points as 'the ambiguity of an equivocal word'.

[7] Literally "*a calling back*" and refers here to one word used in two different ways in the same place.

own,' even all things that he had made, 'καί οἱ ἴδιοι and his own,' i.e. the greatest part of the people, 'received him not.' So again John 3.6, 'That which is born of the Spirit, is spirit:' 'Spirit' in the first place is the almighty Spirit of God, in the latter, a spiritual life of grace received from him. Now in such places as these to argue, that such is the signification of the word in one place, therefore in the other, were violently to pervert the mind of the Holy Ghost. Thus also is the word 'world' usually changed in the meaning thereof: So John 1.10, 'He was in the world, and the world was made by him, and the world knew him not:' He that should force the same signification upon the word in that triple mention of it, would be an egregious glosser, for in the first, it plainly signifieth some part of the habitable Earth, and is taken *subjectivè* μερικῶς;[8] in the second, the whole frame of Heaven and Earth, and is taken *subjectivè*, ὁλικῶς;[9] and in the third, for some men living in the earth, viz. unbelievers, who may be said to be the world *adjunctivè*. So again John 3.17, 'God sent not his Son into the world to condemn the world, but that the world through him might be saved:' Where by the 'world' in the first is necessarily to be understood, that part of the habitable world wherein our savior conversed; in the second, all men in the world, as some suppose, so also there is a truth in it, for our savior came not to condemn all men in the world; for first, condemnation of any was not the prime aim of his coming; secondly, he came to save his own people, and so not to condemn all; in the third, God's Elect, or believers living in the world in their several generations, are meant (although it is granted, they are not considered in this place as Elect, but under such a notion

---

[8] *"Partially."*
[9] *"Wholly, universally."*

as being true of them, serves for the farther exaltation of God's love towards them, which is the end here designed; and this is, as they are poor miserable lost creatures, in the world, of the world, scattered abroad in all places of the world, not tied to Jews or Greeks, but dispersed in any nation, kindred, or language under Heaven: *ex eod.*[10] pg. 201, the like is to be said of parallel texts), who were they whom he intended to save, and none else, or he faileth of his purpose, and the endeavor of Christ is insufficient for the accomplishing of that, whereunto it is designed.

Secondly, that no argument can be taken from a phrase of speech in the Scripture in any particular place, if in other places thereof, where it is used, the signification pressed from that place is evidently denied, unless the scope of the place or subject matter do inforce it: For instance, God is said to love the world, and send his Son; to be in Christ reconciling the world to himself, and Christ to be a propitiation for the sins of the whole world: If the scope of the places where these assertions are, or the subject matter of which they treat, will inforce an universality of all persons to be meant by the word 'world;' so let it be without control: But if not; if there be no inforcement of any such interpretation from the places themselves [as indeed there is not, but the contrary, that being spoken in them concerning the world, viz. their being loved of God, reconciled to him, forgiven, &c., that in other texts is plainly denied to be the portion of all and every person in the world], why should the world there more signify, all and every one, than in John 1.10, 'The world knew him not,' which if it be meant of all without exception, then no one did believe in Christ, contrary to v. 12 or in Luke 2.1, 'that all the world should be taxed;' when none

---

[10] "*From that.*"

but the chief inhabitants of the Roman Empire can be understood: Or in John 8.26, 'I speak to the world those things which I have heard of him,' understanding the Jews to whom he spoke, who then lived in the world, and not everyone to whom he was not sent: Or in John 12.19, 'Perceive ye not that the world is gone after him?' which world was nothing but a great multitude of one small nation, &c.

That all nations, an expression of equal extent with that of the world, is in like manner to be understood, is apparent, Rom. 1.5; Rev. 18.3, 23; Psalm 118.10; 1 Chron. 14.17; Jer. 27.7. It being evident that the words 'world,' 'all the world,' 'the whole world,' where taken adjunctively for men in the world, usually, and almost always ways denote only some, or many men in the world, distinguished into good or bad, believers or unbelievers, elect or reprobate; by what is immediately in the several places affirmed of them: I see no reason in the world why they should be wrested, to any other meaning or sense, in the places that are in controversy between us and our opponents.

Now as we have said of the word 'world,' so we may of the word 'all,' wherein much strength is placed, and many causeless boastings are raised from it: That it is nowhere affirmed in the Scripture, that Christ died for 'all men,' or gave himself a ransom for all men, much less for all and every man, we have before declared: That he gave himself a ransom for all, is expressly affirmed, 2 Tim. 2.6. But now who this 'all' should be, whether all believers, or all the Elect, or some of all sorts, or all of every sort, is in debate. Our adversaries affirm the last, and the main reason they bring to assert their interpretation, is from the importance of the word itself, for that the circumstances of the place, the analogy of faith, and other helps for exposition, do not at all favor their gloss, we shall show when we come to the particular places urged: For the present let us look upon the word in its usual acceptation in the Scripture, and search whether it always necessarily requires such an interpretation.

That the word *all* being spoken of among all sorts of men, speaking, writing, any way expressing themselves but especially in holy writ, is to be taken either collectively, for all in general without exception, or distributively for some of all sorts, excluding none, is more apparent than that it can require any illustration. That it is sometimes taken in the first sense for all collectively is granted, and I need not prove it, they whom we oppose, affirming that this is the only sense of the word, though I dare boldly say, it is not one in ten times so to be understood in the usage of it through the whole book of God; but that it is commonly, and indeed properly used in the latter sense, for some of all sorts, concerning whatsoever it is affirmed; a few instances for many that might be urged, will make it clear. Thus then ye have it John 12.32. 'And I, if I be lifted up from the earth, will draw all unto me:' That we translate it 'all men,' as in other places (for though I know the sense may be the same, yet the word men being not in the original, but only πάντας[11]) I cannot approve. But who I pray are these all? Are they all and everyone? Then are all and every one drawn to Christ, made believers, and truly converted, and shall be certainly saved, for those that come unto him by his, and his Father's drawing, 'he will in no wise cast out,' John 6.37. All then, can here be no other than many, some of all sorts, no sort excluded, according as the word is interpreted, Rev. 5.9, 'Thou hast redeemed us out of every

---

[11] "*All*."

kindred, tongue, and people, and nation:' These are the 'all' he draws to him; which exposition of this phrase is with me of more value and esteem, than a thousand glosses of the children of men. So also Luke 11.42, where our translators have made the word to signify immediately and properly (for translators are to keep close to the proper and native signification of every word) what we assert to be the right interpretation of it; for they render πᾶν λάχανον which ῥητῶς,[12] is every herb; 'all manner of herbs,' taking the word (as it must be) distributively for herbs of all sorts, and not for every individual herb, which the Pharisees did not, could not tithe. In the very same sense is the word used again, Luke 18.12,[13] 'I give tithe of all that I have;' where it cannot signify every individual thing, as is apparent: Most evident also is this restrained signification of the word, Acts 2.17, 'I will pour out of my Spirit ἐπὶ πᾶσαν σάρκα[14] upon all flesh;' which whether it compriseth every man or no, let every man judge; and not rather men of several and sundry sorts: The same course of interpretation as formerly, is followed by our translators, Acts 10.12, rendering πάντα τὰ τετράποδα[15] literally 'all beasts;' or 'four-footed creatures;' 'all manner of beasts;' or 'beasts of sundry several sorts:' In the same sense also must it be understood, Rom. 14.2, 'One believeth that he may eat all things,' i.e. what he pleaseth of things to be eaten of; see moreover 1 Cor. 1.5, yea in that very chapter[16]

---

[12] *"Every herb," "literally."*
[13] Luke 18.11 in original.
[14] *"On all flesh."*
[15] *"All four-footed creatures."*
[16] In the 1648 edition of *The Death of Death* (and followed by Coxe), this sentence does not make proper sense. The 1649 edition, published as part of John Owen, *Certain Treatises* (London: Philemon Stephens, 1649) corrects what was obviously a type-setting error. The corrected sentence reads "Yea in that very chapter where men so eagerly contend that the word *All* is to be taken for all and every one (though fruitlessly and falsely, as shall be demonstrated) *viz.* 1 *Tim.* 2.4 where it is said, that God would have all men to be saved, in

(confessedly) the word is to be expounded according to the sense we give, viz. v. 8, 'I will therefore that men pray ἐν παντὶ τόπῳ[17] which that it cannot signify every individual place in Heaven, Earth and Hell, is of all confessed, and needs no proof.

I shall conclude all concerning these general expressions that are used in the Scripture about this business, in these observations.

First, the word 'all' is certainly and unquestionably sometimes restrained, to all of some sorts, although the qualification be not expressed, which is the bond of the limitation: So for all believers in 1 Cor. 15.22; Eph. 4.10; Rom. 5.18. The free gift came upon all men to the Justification of life; which all men that are so actually justified, are no more nor less, than those that are Christ's, i.e. believers, for certainly Justification is not without faith.

Secondly, the word 'all' is sometimes used for some of all sorts, Jer. 31.34, the word כֻּלָּם is by Paul rendered πάντες, Heb. 8.11, so John 12.32; 1 Tim. 2.1-3, which is made apparent by the mention of kings as one sort of people there intended. And I make no doubt but it will appear to all, that the word must be taken in one of these senses in every place where it is used in the business of redemption.

Thirdly, let a diligent comparison be made, between the general expressions of the new, with the predictions of the Old Testament, and they will be found to be answerable to, and expository of one another. The Lord affirming in the New that, that was done, which in the Old

---

that very chapter (confessedly) the word is to be expounded according to the sense we give, *viz.* v. 8 ...." This is an example of haplography, in which the type-setter omitted the phrases between the two instances of "in that very chapter." The Banner of Truth edition includes the omitted phrases.

[17] *"In every place."*

he foretold should be done: Now in the predictions and prophecies of the Old Testament (that all nations, all people, all flesh, all the ends, families or kindreds of the Earth, the world, the whole Earth, the isles, shall be converted, look up to Christ, come to the mountain of the Lord, and the like) none doubts but that the Elect of God in all nations are only signified, knowing that in them alone those predictions have the truth of their accomplishments: And why should the same expressions used in the Gospel, and many of them aiming directly to declare the fulfilling the other, be wire-drawn to a larger extent, so contrary to the mind of the Holy Ghost?

In fine, as when the Lord is said to wipe tears from all faces, it hinders not but the reprobates shall be cast out to eternity, where there is weeping and wailing, &c. So when Christ is said to die for all, it hinders not but those reprobates may perish to eternity for their sins, without any effectual remedy intended for them, though occasionally proposed to some of them.

Thus far are the words of that worthy servant of Christ.

I shall now return to Mr. Collier.
The Scriptures that he produceth to prove that Christ died for all men (viz. Judas as well as Peter; those that were already under divine vengeance when he laid down his life, as well as those that were saved), are these, John 1.29; 1 Tim. 2.6; Heb. 2.9; 1 John 2.2; 2 Cor. 5.19. He tells us not how he thinks to inforce his notion by them, but takes it for granted, that the word "**world**," and "**all**" used in them must intend every individual person in the world, which hypothesis is abundantly overthrown in the foregoing lines; and there needs no farther answer to them; only I will briefly clear Heb. 2.9, that there may be no occasion of stumbling left to any. The words are thus translated, "**That he by the grace of God should taste death for**

every man:" The word in the Greek is ὑπὲρ παντός "for everyone;" which is here used for ὑπὲρ πάντων "for all." That this term "every man" is commonly used in Scriptures where some limitation of it must be allowed is certain, see [Col. 1.28] [The original mistakenly reads Col. 1.21], where "every man" can intend only those to whom Paul preached, and 1 Cor. 12.7 with chapters 4 and 5. And in this chapter we have such a description of these "**all**" for whom Christ tasted death, as will by no means agree to all and every one, but the Elect only, v. 10; they are called many sons to be brought to glory, v. 11; his brethren and those that are sanctified, the children that God gave him, v. 13; those that were delivered from slavish fear of death, v. 15. I conclude therefore that the "**all**" here spoken of are all Christ's sheep and they only, whether Jews or Gentiles, &c.

Mr. Collier seems to be aware, that he hath made very bold with the two last texts cited by him, and that they will not bear the sense he imposeth upon them; and therefore he states an objection against his application of them to the general ransom, pg. 14. And seeing he will have it brought in, I will take leave to frame the objection myself (and know that the like might be urged with reference to the other texts).

By the "**world**" in 2 Cor. 5.19, and the "**whole world**," 1 John 2.2, we may not understand all and every man in the world, because that which is affirmed in these texts, is not applicable to them; in Corinthians those that are called "**the world**" in v. 19 are called us (believers) v. 18. They are reconciled to God, and have the pardon, or are under the non-imputation of their sins, being made the righteousness of God in Christ: So also those spoken of in John were such whose sins Christ was a propitiation for, and that had by him interest in the favor of God; so that in both these Scriptures, actual reconciliation to God, and the application of grace rather than the impetration thereof is intended, in which, multitudes in the world have no part; and therefore these terms can intend no more, but men living throughout the whole world in all the parts and regions thereof (in opposition to the inhabitants of any one country or place as such) even so many of them as being ordained to eternal life did believe, as well Gentiles as Jews; according to John 11.51-52.

That Mr. Collier acquits himself but poorly in his answer to the objection as framed by himself, everyone will see, that shall seriously weigh his lines. The sum of what he insists on is this;

> *"That the Scripture clearly states a general reconciliation, and a special: A general reconciliation of all things, all men, Col. 1.20."* And having made peace by the blood of his cross to reconcile all things to himself, whether things in Earth, or things in Heaven, &c. *"A special reconciliation of believers, which is not the same as the general, but ariseth out of it, and is that intended Col. 1.21. Both these we have likewise in Rom. 5.8, 10."*

These texts do in no wise prove what Mr. Collier doth produce them for. The first mentioned, viz. Col. 1.20, is by divers learned and judicious men, interpreted according to the subject matter, "all things," i.e. the whole Church or family of God; in Heaven, viz. "the spirits of just men made perfect;" and in Earth, i.e. the Elect still in the world, even all that are reconciled, are so in Christ. And if he carry it farther, as some able interpreters do also; and will have angels included, and also the fabric of Heaven and Earth, and the creatures therein made for the service of man, yet can it not on a like account be applied to all these, we cannot rightly conceive of a reconciliation of angels (properly so called) that never sinned, it is at most but an analogical reconciliation, they being confirmed in grace, and secured in their station by Christ. And so with respect to the things that are in the world; it can be but a metaphorical reconciliation, for they never sinned, neither was God angry with them as breakers of his Law which they were not made under: Indeed as God commanded that all that did belong to Achan should be destroyed for his sin, so we may conceive, that the whole Creation that was made for man's use, came under a curse for his sake, and for the farther declaration of God's hatred of sin, must have perished with him, had it not been for the mediator; and so Christ keeps off the wrath that was pouring forth upon man, and all his substance (if I may so say). But this comes much short of Mr. Collier's purpose, and is so far from proving any special reconciliation arising out of the general, that it is from hence manifest, that the last mentioned is a fruit and adjunct of the first. Indeed this text, and that in the Romans, holds forth no more than this, that by the death of Christ all the Elect of God were virtually, and fundamentally reconciled to him, while they were sinners, i.e. the price of their redemption was then paid down to God, and accepted by him; but the actual application of it to their souls, and their personal interest in it is upon believing: It is also evident that (especially) the text last mentioned, doth hold forth the certain application of the grace purchased and obtained by Christ's death unto all those for whom he died, which quite overthrows Mr. Collier's notion of the general ransom.

He proceeds, pg. 15, to question,

> "In what sense may the world be said to be reconciled to God, and to have sin not imputed? He means, not to have sin imputed."

I answer not in his sense, for if we understand by the world, as he doth, the whole universe: To talk of the reconciliation of birds and beasts, stones and trees, &c. unto God without any distinction, and the non-imputation of sin unto them that were never under any law, is absurd and foolish: No nor yet is it true in respect of all and every one of the sons of men in the world, for the greatest part of them live and die enemies in their minds to God, they are **children of wrath by nature,** Eph. 2.3, and lie "ἐν τῷ πονηρῷ[18] **in the wicked one,**" 1 John 5.19, "**and the wrath of God abideth on them,**" John 3.36. But Mr. Collier saith, they are so in a twofold respect:

---

[18] *"In the wicked one."*

1. "They are so far reconciled and sin not imputed, as to have the Gospel of reconciliation truly tendered to them, that whosoever do accept it on the same terms thereof might be reconciled and saved."

This answer is built upon his supposition, that the Gospel ought to be, and is preached to all inanimate and animate creatures as well as man; the folly of which notion I shall farther detect by and by: At present I make my reply only with regard unto men, and even with respect to them, it is exceeding short and weak. *"Reconciliation is tendered,"* saith he, *"to the world; and pardon of sin is offered on Gospel terms:"* Grant it, doth this prove that they are already reconciled and pardoned? But indeed the Gospel is not preached to all men in the world.

2. "The word is so far reconciled and sin not imputed, as that it shall not hinder their resurrection, and restitution out of the fallen state, 1 Cor. 15.22; Acts 3.21."

If there be in these words any due coherence with what Mr. Collier writes before, then doth he here present us with another new notion, of the resurrection of all those creatures that died, or shall die, before the restoration of the universe; but then certainly the world must not only be restored, but either new made or greatly enlarged, otherwise there will not be found therein place for them all. But however two things with reference to man he supposeth undoubted,

1. "That all men are by the death of Christ recovered from their fallen state," &c.

What he intends hereby, he doth not explain; and it is too evident that he little understands what the redemption and recovery of man out of his lost and lapsed state means. I cannot understand by what mediums he will prove, that the world of ungodly men, that lie in their filth and under their guilt, that are estranged from the womb, and speak lies as soon as they are born, with whom God is angry every day, and they die in their sins, are yet reconciled to God and restored from their fallen state: When he hath done it,

— *Erit mihi magnus Apollo.*[19]

For the present we have only his word for it, without any proof tendered.

> *2. "That the resurrection of all men (vessels of wrath as well as vessels of mercy) is a fruit of their being reconciled to God by Christ."*

Now seeing the wicked are raised for no other end, but that they may be brought to a just, though fearful, Judgment, and are raised immortal that they may be capable of enduring the fire that shall never be quenched, I cannot see that this is any proof of their being redeemed by Christ, more than the devils, that must also receive their sentence from him in that day. And whereas he cites 1 Cor. 15.22, it gives no countenance to his notion: The Apostle saith indeed, v. 21, that **"By Christ came the resurrection from the dead**," and v. 22, that **"all shall be made alive in him**:" But who are these all? All and every one of the sons of men? No certainly; for to **"be made alive"** in this text, doth not signify simply the resurrection of the body, in which the wicked have a share also, but their resurrection to a blessed immortality, to bear his image who is the Lord from Heaven, confer v. 45–50. In this context Adam and Christ are opposed as two public persons; and the term **"all"** is to be expounded accordingly: All that

---

[19] *"He will be to me a great Apollo"* i.e. as great as Apollo. This is an adaptation of a line from Virgil's *Eclogues* 3.104 *"eris mihi magnus Apollo"* – 'you will be to me a great Apollo'. Coxe seems to say "If Collier can [prove the above], then he must have the insight of Apollo [the god of prophecy]."

were in Adam as their head and representative, died in him when he fell, and so all that were in Christ as their head and representative, shall be made alive in and by him; even all us, believers, they that are Christ's, of whom he is the first fruits, v. 23. And indeed throughout this chapter the Apostle manifests, that it is the happy and joyful resurrection of the saints that he is speaking of, and all his reasoning thereabout is accordingly suited to such: And it is granted, that the redeemed of the Lord have a resurrection unto life and glory, by virtue of their interest in Christ, who died and rose again: So then the resurrection considered as the spring of believers' happiness, and their glorious privilege, came by Christ: But how Mr. Collier will evince that there is the like reason to refer the resurrection of the wicked, which is only unto condemnation, unto their redemption by Christ, I see not. He proceeds:

> "—And the second death shall be for sin against the New Covenant and Gospel law of grace, for not accepting the reconciliation and salvation on the terms thereof, John 3.19."

If there be any kind of argument in these words to Mr. Collier's purpose, it must be this:

> *If Christ had not died for all men, and reconciliation to God by him been tendered to them on Gospel-terms, they had not been liable to the second death. But all that do not believe and obey the Gospel, must die the second death, Ergo, Christ died for them, and procured non-imputation of sin to them, &c.*

I deny the major proposition: Sinners are guilty of damnation by the breach of the Law, though they never hear the Gospel, &c.

And immediately Thomas Collier will deny the minor, as we shall hear: Certainly he will be hard put to it to prove that all men are redeemed, because most men are damned.

The Scripture cited by him, viz. John 3.19, proves indeed, that where the objective light of the Gospel is afforded to a people, and they obey it not, but refuse to walk in it, they shall die the second death, yea their case will be worse than others that have not enjoyed the like means: Unbelief is a crying sin, and brings them under condemnation with a witness (as we use to speak). But it doth in no wise prove, what Mr. Collier supposeth, that none are guilty of the second death, by the breach of the first Covenant.

And in plain terms Mr. Collier doth not think, that all that have not faith in Christ shall be damned, as his minor proposition supposeth; though for the present he is willing to pretend so, that he may thereby prove they are redeemed; for thus he writes, pg. 26:

> *Damnation is the judgment of Gospel-unbelief and disobedience [he intends that only], yet those that never heard the Gospel cannot be under this judgment, because it is impossible (without a miracle) that they should believe the Gospel, it is in some sense their affliction and judgment that they have it not; but not their sin because they believe it not because they cannot, Rom. 10.14.*

I grant that a law cannot oblige, unless it be sufficiently made known or published, and that there are multitudes in the word that enjoy not the Gospel; and these, as they are (in an ordinary way) capable of no saving benefit by Christ; so neither is the sin of not believing the Gospel chargeable upon them. But even these are under the first covenant, which requires of them perfect obedience to the moral law, or law of nature, which (if they have not the written Law neither) is so far written, even in their hearts, as that they are a law unto themselves, and utterly inexcusable in the breach of it, Rom. 1.19-20; 2.15.[20] But amongst these "**there are many filled with all**

---

[20] Why those who have not the Gospel are condemned.

unrighteousness," ch. 1, v. 21-31. And shall we suppose according to this man's licentious doctrine, that these are in danger only of a temporal death, which the best in the world cannot escape? The consciences of these very wretches tell them otherwise, v. 32, where by death, the second death, or perishing under divine wrath must be understood, otherwise there were no evil peculiar to them intended therein; and the Apostle assures us, that "**the wrath of God is revealed from Heaven against all unrighteousness and ungodliness of men,**" who imprison and stifle their natural light, holding that truth in unrighteous, and not subjecting themselves thereto, through the enmity that is in their hearts to God, v. 18, &c. Though the law cannot give life; yet is its curse heavy enough, to sink all the world under eternal wrath, which it had done without remedy, if Christ had not delivered believers from the curse of the Law by being made a curse for them, Gal. 3.13.

Thus we have heard out Mr. Collier what he hath to say for the reconciliation of all the world to God, and the non-imputation of sin to them; and I know some will take notice of that which immediately follows in the next section, where he asserts,

That "*there is a more special design of grace in the death of Christ, i.e. the salvation of his Elect of his Church, whose peculiar privilege it is, that the blood of Christ is shed for them for the remission of sin:*" And they will perhaps wonder at the man's acumen, that hath found out such a notable distinction of non-imputation of sin; from remission of sin; the one of which belongeth to the reprobate, the other to the Elect; though Paul took them to be of the same import, Rom. 4.7-8. But I cannot stay to remark every absurdity in his book; and therefore let this pass.

The glorious and wonderful design of free grace to redeem and save to the utmost all the Elect, by Jesus Christ, I adore: And to own that there was any end or design of God in the death of his Son, which was not perfectly accomplished thereby I dare not: But I shall proceed with Mr. Collier, it not being my purpose (as I said at first) to enter upon a full discussion of these points, or to urge the arguments that might be pleaded against his opinion, but only to clear our way of that rubbish that he hath cast into it.

He discourseth in the next place of the preaching of the Gospel, and he is as liberal here (and good reason for it) as he was in determining the extent of Christ's death.

> *"The design of God,"* saith he, *"in his Gospel grace by the death of his Son, being thus universal to the whole world in this threefold sense as hath been mentioned; hence it is that the Gospel must be preached to the whole Creation,"* &c. He grants indeed pg. 16, that *"It is especially to be published to men who were concerned in the sin and fall, but it is and may be truly preached to the whole Creation, though they hear it not, nor understand it."*

I suppose in this particular, Mr. Collier may truly say he hath not followed authors, for I know none before him that have been so fond as to assert what here he doth; though in other things it is evident that he hath imbibed the notions of divers heretics that have been before him. Although I must confess the Papists in some of their legends tell many odd stories to this purpose, and we may collect from thence what some of them thought in this matter. And although all Protestants deride their foppery; that will not discourage Mr. Collier from joining with them in this and other things, for he hath observed (as he tells us, pg. 59) that *"The Protestants run themselves too much in both principle and practice, beyond (almost) all works of charity;"* amongst which perhaps he reckons preaching to birds and beasts, stones and trees, &c.

If I should recite to Mr. Collier some of the stories they tell of St. Francis his preaching oft to the birds, and how affectionately they heard him, his converting a ravenous wolf, from his rapine to a tame and harmless life, &c., and of Father Bede his preaching to the stones, when he was blind, and his naughty boy led him to a heap of stones instead of a company of men, and how in the close of his devotion they all cried out with a loud voice "Amen." How he would approve of these things I know not; but others would think I intended to make him ridiculous; and therefore I will forbear; only if he will allow me freely to impart my thoughts with him, I shall say this, that I think Mr. Collier would have been much more innocently employed, if he had thus spent his time, and never preached and printed to men the lamentable stuff that we have in this book.

But let us consider what proof of this notion he offers to us.

There are two Scriptures produced by him, Mark 16.15 and Col. 1.23. The first saith, "**Go ye into all the world and preach the Gospel to every creature**:" Concerning which he tells us,

> "*The word translated 'to every creature,' is in the Greek to all the Creation;* πάσῃ τῇ κτίσει, *to all the Creation.*"

What emphasis Mr. Collier supposeth in these words "*to all the Creation,*" more than in these "to every creature," I know not: Some great thing he hath imagined in this criticism that nobody else can find out, else he would not have inculcated it with such a tautology as he doth: Or it may be he only took this occasion to show his skill in the Greek: But if that be it, I must beg his pardon, for I think it is not much learning, but something else, that hath made him so far forget himself as to interpret this Scripture after such a manner as he hath. There is doubtless no more intended in Mark than is in other words expressed by Matthew in his record of the same commission; "**Go ye therefore and teach all nations, baptizing them,**" &c. Matt. 28.19-20. So that the commission to preach the Gospel to every creature, intends only those concerned to hear and obey it; as the following words evince, "**He that believeth and is baptized shall be saved**," &c. even the children of men of all nations, kindreds and tongues, as well as the Jews. And as this phrase suits our dialect or way of speaking, in the same sense; so was it common with the Jews (as I could evince from their writings) to use the word in their language, that properly signifieth a creature for a man, because men are the most excellent of all visible creatures.

Of the same import is Col. 1.23. But there the words are expressly, which was preached "ἐν πάσῃ τῇ κτίσει τῇ ὑπὸ τὸν οὐρανόν, **in all the Creation that is under Heaven**," i.e. in all the Earth to the men that dwell thereon. But Mr. Collier saith that "under Heaven" may be understood to be "under God:" I answer it may not, neither is this phrase, "under Heaven," so to be expounded anywhere in the Scripture; and although it be allowed that in the texts cited by him, "Heaven" is put for "God;" yet it is so used not according to its proper signification, but figuratively per *metonymiam adjuncti*,[21] for "him that dwells in Heaven." It doth not therefore follow that we may take it in that sense wherever we meet with it. But what he means by this I know not, unless he would have the Gospel preached not only to the whole visible Creation, but also to the devils, for they are under God. Neither know I what to make of that which follows:

> *That the Gospel may be truly preached to the whole Creation, though they hear it not, nor understand it: And thus we must understand Col. 1.23. For the Gospel was not then preached in the hearing of all men, nor in the hearing of the whole Creation, yet it was preached to all the Creation.*

If this were true, the Apostles needed not to have gone abroad into the world to have preached the Gospel to every creature; but I am persuaded if one at London should pretend that he daily preached the Gospel to the Turks in Constantinople that hear him not, or to the animate and inanimate creatures that either are not capable of hearing or understanding what he saith; many would laugh at his folly, and conclude the man was under a delirium; but none would think that he truly preached the Gospel to any of these, nor yet that

---

[21] A metonymy in which one word is substituted for another closely related word. In this case, *heaven* stands for *God*.

it was worth their while to refute his conceit by argument. Yea but thus we must understand Col. 1.23. Mr. Collier were doubtless the greatest tyrant in the world, if he could force our understandings to assent to so great an absurdity: But his words are but wind, we have our liberty still to think otherwise; especially seeing his reason for it is so weak. "*For*," saith he, "*though the Gospel was not then preached in the hearing of all the Creation, yet it was preached to all the Creation:*" which in plain terms amounts to no more than this: It must be so because Thomas Collier saith it was so.

This needs no answer, *valeat quantum valere potest*.[22] We may conclude, this notwithstanding, that the Gospel was preached in the hearing of all it was preached to.

In the next place he tells us, that "*The work of God do preach the Gospel to the whole Creation.*" His notion of "*The preaching of the Gospel by the works of God,*" we shall meet with again, and farther examine presently: In the meantime we might inquire what these works of God are that preach to the whole Creation in his sense; for surely the works of God that preach, must not be the same with the whole Creation preached to: But, however Mr. Collier escape for writing thus; I should incur the censure of idleness if I should pursue so fruitless an inquiry. I will therefore leave it off; and proceed to the doubt or question that he moves, and endeavors to solve pg. [16].[23]

> Question: "*If Christ died for the sins of the world, and if God had a real design of good will and grace to all men, in his general love, why then is not the Gospel preached to all men? Whence is it that the greatest part of the world have been, and still are without the Gospel?*"

If Mr. Collier had not been conscious to himself that his previous discourse had been very vain and futilous, he needed not to have moved this doubt; having already concluded, "*that a man may preach*

---

[22] This is a legal phrase, literally "let it have effect as far as it can have effect."
[23] The original cites page 17, but Collier's question begins on page 16 of his *Additional Word*.

the Gospel to the whole Creation, though they hear him not, nor understand him;" and that it is also "*preached to all by the works of God.*" But the truth is, notwithstanding all he hath said or can say, there is great weight in what he here suggests. For certainly if Christ had given himself a ransom for all men, seeing none can enjoy the benefit thereof without faith, and none can believe on him, of whom they have not heard; he would not so have disposed things in his providence, that multitudes of these ransomed ones should never have knowledge thereof: But we see that things are so ordered, ergo, he never intended to give himself a ransom for all men, in Mr. Collier's sense. Let us hear what Mr. Collier saith to these things.

The first branch of his answer to this inquiry, as proposed by himself, hath nothing in it but a repetition of his former error, about the present recovery of all men out of their fallen state; which hath already on good grounds been rejected; and he here gives it no inforcement: He adds:

> 2. "*The Gospel hath been and still is preached to the whole world by the works of God, and his common goodness to men, Psalm 19.1-2; Rom. 10.18; Psalm 145.8-9; Rom. 2.4.*"

The question is about that preaching of the Gospel that is a sufficient means to beget faith, and so infers the duty of those to whom it is so preached to believe and obey it; that it is so preached by the works of God, Mr. Collier in this treatise flatly denies: We recited one passage to this purpose but a little before: I cannot think therefore that he at all satisfies his own conscience in this answer; but only to serve a turn, thrusts in this notion to amuse his ignorant reader. He doth not at all explain himself in what sense he supposeth the works of God preach the Gospel: Indeed his notion is utterly false, and therefore we need not wait for his explication of it; neither do the Scriptures quoted by him prove any such thing: By the works of God, we grant, his eternal power and Godhead is knowable to the sons of men, which leaves them without excuse in that they worship him not as God: And by his common goodness, is his patience and long-suffering of the vessels of wrath manifested, which is a further witness against them in their impenitency and rebellion against him: And this is all the Scriptures produced by Mr. Collier speak: There is not a word of preaching the Gospel in any of them; except in Rom. 10.18, which is not by the works of God, but by a ministry sent forth from God for that work, as the whole context doth manifest, which is also quoted by Mr. Collier to prove that none can believe without that means; notwithstanding this supposed preaching of the works of God. So then though the Apostle apply those words in Psalm 19 to his present purpose, either by allusion to them, or more directly; yet doth he in no wise teach that the Heavens, Sun, &c. preach the Gospel, but rather the contrary. In Psalm 19 there is mention made of a double medium of the revelation of God to the sons of men, viz. his works, and his Word: What the works of God teach, and what the efficacy of their teaching is, the Apostle discourseth Rom. 1.19, *ad finem*.[24] Unto the word of God the Psalmist ascribeth much more; even all saving effects, v. 7-11, and herein its excellency beyond the other is manifested. He proceeds:

> 3. "*Though there is no other name given under Heaven among men whereby they may be saved, Acts 4.12, yet we must own that many have been, and may be saved by that name, that never heard of him, and so could not have faith in him.*"

In this it must be granted that Mr. Collier speaks to the purpose, and hath said something that gives real countenance to his notions, and directly overthrows that which hath generally been the received doctrine of the Protestants, yea razeth the foundation of Gospel grace, and therefore here we might have expected some formidable arguments to drive Christians from that stronghold of their common

---

[24] "*To the end.*"

faith, "That believing in Christ is the only way to glory." But how miserably he falters in his proof notwithstanding his strange confidence, we shall immediately discern. I desire the reader to bear in mind, that persons adult, and endued with reason, are the subjects of this discourse. Mr. Collier's drift then is to show, that although it would grate upon this notion, that all the world should not hear of Christ, if there were no other way to be saved by him, but believing in him, yet it is otherwise, if many may be saved by him, without faith in him, which they could not have but by hearing. And that many have, and may be saved without that, we "*must own.*" Dictator like! But why must we own it? Because if we will not own this, Thomas Collier cannot prove that all men are redeemed. And verily if we do own it, we must directly contradict the Apostle, who saith, that **"Without faith it is impossible to please God,"** Heb. 11.6. And that he there intends believing in God by Christ, in whom alone we can know him to be a rewarder of all that diligently seek him, the whole scope of that chapter doth manifest; and if Mr. Collier think meet to deny it, I shall God assisting, evince the certainty thereof, beyond his contradiction. And as he at present doth not, so I am assured he, nor his companions with him, cannot produce one text of Scripture that gives countenance to his notion.

That kind of proof which he offers, I will now consider.

> *"For,"* saith he, *"we may not suppose that any shall die the second death for not believing in the Son of God as crucified, that never heard of him, Rom. 10.14."*

What there is in these words that may any ways strengthen his notion, I cannot imagine: The argument is this:

> *"None shall die the second death"* for not believing, *"which have not heard of Christ:"*
> *"But many that have not heard of him do die the second death:"* Ergo, *"many may be saved without faith in him."*

I hope by this kind of arguing he will not infect many with his principles; we have already said and proved, that though disobedience to the Gospel, be not chargeable on those that never heard it, yet are they under the curse of God's holy Law, and must die the second death, for their breach thereof, seeing they remain strangers to the only remedy: And in the discourse of the Apostle cited by him, he supposeth, that there is no salvation to be had without calling upon the Lord; no calling upon the Lord without faith, no faith without hearing; Ergo, without hearing no salvation. He goes on:

> *And we must likewise understand, that there hath been a sufficiency of teaching, under all the ministries of God to the world, to bring them to the knowledge of God, and so to salvation by that name (though unknown to them), and to leave all others without excuse, which could not be were there not a sufficiency of teaching therein, Rom. 1.19-21; 2.1.*

Here we have Mr. Collier again (as if he conceited himself in St. Peter's chair) imposing his magisterial dictates upon us: This we must know, and that we must understand; but no warranty thereof tendered besides his αὐτὸς ἔφη;[25] and though perhaps he will take it amiss that his authority is rejected, and may think with himself, *Si hoc non fit probationum satis, nescio quid sit satis*;[26] yet I shall peremptorily deny, and prove the contrary to, what he here asserts, and supposeth undeniable, viz.

1. "*That there is a saving knowledge of God attainable out of Christ.*" This is first, contrary to the whole tenor of the Scripture, that represents God as a consuming fire to all that are out of Christ; a God that will by no means clear the guilty;

---

[25] "*He himself has spoken*" i.e. he presents himself as an authority so that the reader ought simply to take his word alone.
[26] "*If this proof is not sufficient, I do not know what will be.*"

and that his pardoning love and grace is made known to the sons of men only in and by the mediator; life and immortality is brought to light by the Gospel, and thus it was from the beginning, the foundation of the Church, after the fall of man was laid in the promise of sending Christ to be its savior, &c. There is no knowledge of God saving, but that whereby we know him to be a just God and a savior; and this we cannot know but in and through Christ, who was set forth to be a propitiation through faith in his blood.

Secondly, it is against the express testimony of Christ, John 14.6, "**I am the way, the truth, and the life; no man cometh unto the Father but by me.**" And again ch. 17.3, "**This is life eternal to know thee the only true God, and Jesus Christ whom thou hast sent into the world,**" not to know God and be ignorant of Christ, as Mr. Collier dreameth: And 1 Pet. 1.20-21, where the efficacy, and saving fruit of Christ's death is declared to belong only to those who by him do believe in God, and that it is God considered as raising him from the dead, and giving him glory (so testifying his acceptance of the price that Christ paid for the redemption of sinners) that is the object of our faith and hope. More might be added, but I hasten.

Thirdly, it is also contrary to the experience of all that are saved. There are some proud hypocrites indeed, that are alive without the Law; that think they can please God and trust in him without a mediator; but a poor convinced sinner, unto whom the Commandment is come with powers; and he by it is convinced of the holiness of God, and the exceeding sinfulness of his sin; can find no rest until he have Christ revealed in him; all thoughts of God out of a mediator, are breaking and terrible to him, neither can he put his trust in God, nor dares he once to think of an approach to him, until he have some knowledge of the meeting together of mercy and justice, and how righteousness and peace did kiss each other in the undertaking of a crucified savior.

2. That which he farther supposeth in the words recited is:

"That the works of God without his word, are a sufficient means to bring persons to saving acquaintance with God."

But seeing it is confessed by Mr. Collier that notwithstanding this ministry (as he terms it) of the works of God, men remain under invincible ignorance of Jesus Christ; and we have before proved, that out of Christ there is no saving knowledge of God attainable, there needs no more be said to enervate this proposition also: Only for the more full discovery of its falsehood, observe:

1. In the Old Testament when the Scripture speaks of those nations that enjoyed not the word of God, it speaks of them as people under his wrath, Jer. 10.25, as people neglected of God, and in his just judgment suffered to walk in their own ways, Psalm 147.19-20, compared with Acts 14.16. And the sad effects of being deprived of God's word, we have signally set forth Amos 8.9-14. And in the New Testament when the Apostle relates what condition the Gentiles were in, before they enjoyed the light of the Gospel, he doth it in these words, Eph. 2.12, "**without Christ, aliens from the commonwealth of Israel, and strangers from the covenants of promise: Having no hope, and without God in the world.**" To be brief, though Mr. Collier affirm the contrary; yet the God of truth assures us, "**Where there is no vision the people perish**" Prov. 29.18.

2. The condition of those nations that enjoy not the word of God, is such as plainly bespeaks them to be in the region of the shadow of death: The Apostle discourseth of such Rom.

1.19, &c. and assures us their enmity to God is such, as renders ineffectual the conviction they have of a deity, by his works; and that notwithstanding this means, they grow worse and worse, and necessarily perish at last, if not converted and saved by the grace of Christ revealed in the Gospel, yea, inquire of those that know the state of the poor Indians, and they will fully resolve you, that there is no proof of Mr. Collier's opinion amongst them.

And whereas Mr. Collier saith, that "*Otherwise they were not without excuse*;" the Apostle in the texts cited by him, proves the contrary, showing that they are, and why they are, without excuse. Men are inexcusable in sinning against the Law, and light of nature; yet can none be saved by the works of the Law, without faith in Christ, Gal. 3.10-11.

What he adds in the close of this chapter, that "*God will save all upright hearted ones,*" &c. "*though the special saved ones are such as are espoused to Christ by the Word, Spirit, and faith of the Gospel*;" is a vain flourish, for besides, that its foundation is laid in those principles that have been already disproved, it is a fond imagination, that any are upright hearted with God, or can be so, that are utter strangers to the Word, Spirit, and faith of the Gospel; seeing such must needs remain unconverted, for Mr. Collier himself confesseth, pg. 33, that "*In the great work of conversion, the Spirit worketh in the word of the Gospel, by that means and ministry, and not without it: The Word and Spirit may not be separated, John 3.5; 17.20; James 1.18.*"

CHAPTER IV

Concerning the Moral Power of Man, or Free-Will, where also of Original Sin.

In Mr. Collier's fourth chapter, and that which followeth, he doth abundantly manifest, either great ignorance of the true state of those questions he meddles with, or else a design to pervert their sense that maintain the truths opposed by him, that so he may bring them, and their doctrine under *odium*, and entangle unwary souls with his corrupt notions; to prevent him herein, and to make way for the clear understanding of what I have to say in answer to him, I shall premise these things:

1. That I do acknowledge, that all men have a liberty of will, or freedom of choosing with reference to those things that are proposed to them. And this I take to be an inseparable adjunct of all human acts.

2. This liberty consists in a rational spontaneity: He acts freely, that is under no *coaction* (which alone is opposed to liberty in the true notion thereof) but doth what the last and practical judgment of his own understanding dictates to him. So that one that acts necessarily may yet act most freely. God cannot but love and delight in himself, and order all things to his own glory; yet is he an agent in every respect most absolutely free: The good angels, now confirmed by grace in their station, and glorified saints, cannot but love God, choose and delight in perfect obedience to his holy will: Yet in all this are they free agents, because they are thus determined by no external force, but by the dictate of their own understanding. And on the contrary, the devils, and fallen man, are by their own wickedness determined to sin, and that only, yet are they free in the choice thereof, &c.

3. That God made man upright, and so capable of yielding perfect obedience to the whole will of God, according to that covenant in which he stood related to him; but he sought out many inventions, and by his voluntary defection from, and rebellion against God, fell short of the glory of God, and lost that rectitude of nature which was concreate with him, and became blind, disobedient and dead to God.

4. Man having thus wickedly and willfully lost, and cast away his power of obeying God, doth infer no unrighteousness in the law of God, still requiring and commanding them to do that which is just, and holy, and good; neither doth it infer the least obligation on God to recover him out of his lost estate.

5. Although man in his lapsed estate, hath such a principle of enmity to God reigning in him, that he cannot, until converted by effectual grace, choose that which is right in the sight of God, yet doth he freely put forth a positive act of his

will in refusing mercy tendered on Gospel terms.

6. So then the question is not so much, whether men *left to themselves, and the common helps afforded them, may believe if they will,* but whether any such *will believe*, and not rather finally oppose God, and refuse his grace tendered to them in the Gospel.

These things duly considered, tend to obviate the cavils of Mr. Collier, and to detect his mistakes. He asserts in the first section, pg. 24, that:

> *"Suitable to the means and ministries men are under, there is a capacity both of power and will in all men (that are not debilitated of the ordinary capacities of men) to understand, believe, and obey the Lord in them."*

By this and other following passages, it appears that by universal grace, Thomas Collier means *"the sufficiency of the human nature,"* which is it, and not grace, that he desires to exalt; and as his notions are the same in this matter with the Pelagians, so is there the same deceit and equivocation in his using the term grace, which they sought refuge in: And therefore let none be blinded with that saying of his in the same section, that *"This capacity both of power and will, is of God*;" For Pelagius himself acknowledgeth as much; and it amounts to no more than the acknowledgement of our endowment with natural abilities by God who is our Creator: All these are from God in *a way of nature*, but ability to believe and obey the Gospel is from him in a *way of special grace*, which is that we plead for; and deny that a natural unregenerate man is capable, of saving knowledge of, or yielding obedience to, the will of God in the Gospel, otherwise than as a dead soul is capable of being quickened by the almighty power of the Spirit of Christ. This the Scripture is full and express in: I will instance in a text or two.

We read 1 Cor. 2.14: "**But the natural man receiveth not the things of the Spirit of God; for they are foolishness unto him; neither can he know them, for they are spiritually discerned.**"

The Apostle doth in the context divide all men into two sorts: natural and spiritual. The last have the mind of Christ, and are made acquainted with the grace of the Gospel, through the effectual working of the Spirit, by which they are born again; the other, viz. natural men, unregenerate persons (even the wisest and best of them) "**receive not the things of the Spirit of God,**" i.e. the doctrines of the Gospel; because they are without any spiritual discerning of the glory that is in them, remaining under the power of darkness; they are accounted foolishness, and as foolish things, are slighted and rejected by them: "**Neither can they know them,**" viz. savingly and effectually, "**for they are spiritually discerned,**" i.e. by the enlightening, and teaching of the Spirit of God; and not without it.

But I find divers exceptions laid against this interpretation of the text by Mr. Collier, pg. 42 and 43, which I shall here remove out of the way.

1. He expounds this term "**the natural man**" by "*the sensual man*;" as if all unregenerate persons were not intended thereby, but only some of the most brutish among them; which is quite against the Apostle's scope, whose design is to show, that God hath made foolish the wisdom of this world, and that the principal men thereof are strangers to the things of the New Covenant, "**which eye hath not seen,**" &c. ch. 1.20 & 2.7-9.

2. He supposeth the idolatrous Gentiles that would not come to the Gospel light, &c. to be intended. But this also is plainly to contradict the Apostle, who speaks of both Jew and Gentile, and particularly those of them to whom the Gospel was preached; as you may see most evidently in his foregoing discourse; and these when the things of God's Spirit were

proposed to them, received them not, but esteemed them foolishness.

3. His third exception is plainly ridiculous; he saith, *"All where the Gospel comes should understand and believe it, but it is these only that by the Word and Spirit of the Gospel, do believe and obey it, that have this spiritual understanding."* This we plead, that although all unto whom they are tendered, ought to receive the things of the Spirit of God; yet no unconverted man doth so; the reason is in part, because he cannot understand them, but they are foolishness to him, and accordingly rejected by him; and to confute this, Mr. Collier tells us that no unbeliever hath this understanding indeed; but if he did believe and obey he should have it; as if to obey and believe the Gospel, were not to receive the things of God's Spirit: The sum is this: If he did believe, he might believe, and if he were not ignorant, he might understand, &c.

4. He endeavors to persuade us, that it is only such an understanding of Gospel mysteries as is proper to grown Christians, that the unconverted man is uncapable of, and how repugnant this is to the whole discourse of the Apostle, I leave everyone to judge: Thus he concludes his futilous cavil:

> *"So that it supposeth not any impossibility for the darkest and worst of men to obtain light and life by the Gospel."* He would fain lie hid under the darkness of his ambiguous terms: This Scripture doth not suppose indeed but that the darkest and worst of men, may be enlightened, and quickened, by the power of God's Spirit working with the Word: But that every man, which hath only the natural accomplishments of a man, may understand and obey the Gospel if it be doctrinally proposed to him, in the exercise of that ability which he hath in his lapsed state, is utterly

denied in this text; and Thomas Collier convict thereby of falsehood, who affirms it.

The second Scripture which I shall oppose to his forementioned assertion, is John 6.44, "**No man can come to me except the Father which sent me draw him.**" Christ doth here assert, that notwithstanding the Gospel be preached to men, their natural impotency is such, that they cannot come; yea their enmity such that they will not come, unless the Father draw them, viz. by those effectual teachings, and that illumination, by which alone this impotency is cured in the Elect, v. 45.

Thomas Collier makes his exceptions likewise against this text, pg. 30, but to very little purpose.

1. He endeavors to persuade us that this "**drawing of the Father,**" is the same with the preaching of the Gospel, and so common to all that hear the sound thereof; which the text will in no wise admit, seeing it is of such that hear the Gospel that Christ speaketh, amongst whom some are thus drawn, others not.
2. He saith they cannot, because they will not, and that the one is not without the other. We grant this, they neither can nor will, without special grace come to Christ; neither are men condemned merely for their impotency, but for their willfulness in rejecting the Gospel, but this helps not Mr. Collier at all. And whereas he gives an account in some particulars why they will not, viz.

Because they are habituated in sin, and accustomed to it, &c. And *Because of the influence that the Devil hath upon them: I grant that these things do obstruct and hinder persons from coming to Christ; but I must tell him also, that the first and main reason of their refusal is quite passed over by him, and that is, the natural enmity that is in their souls to God, Rom. 8.7.*

The third Scripture is Eph. 2.1, with other parallel texts that declare all persons unconverted, to be "**dead in trespasses and sins**;" and then certainly uncapable in that condition to put forth any truly spiritual vital act, in receiving and obeying the Gospel of Christ; seeing they are without that principle of life, from whence such acts must flow. Unto this Mr. Collier replies pg. 29:

"*It is a great mistake to think and speak as if men were as dead and uncapable to believe and obey the Gospel, as a stock or a stone, or as men that are naturally dead; this is a ridiculous and untrue imagination:*" And so proceeds with his unlearned eloquence to set forth the folly of giving anything in command to a stone, &c. But to these things I say:

[1][1]All men have indeed rational souls, and none besides Mr. Collier will be so ridiculous as so to talk at such a rate as if men and stones were in the same capacity of being wrought upon by exhortations, promises, and threatenings; we acknowledge that these are proper moral instruments in their own nature suited to work upon the understandings, wills, and affections of men, and to produce the effects of faith and obedience in them; and seeing these faculties are the principle and subject of all actual obedience, it is also granted that there is in men a natural remote passive power of believing and obeying the Gospel which is not in stocks and stones; but this power is never actually put forth, nor can be, without, the effectual grace of God working in them both to will and to do: So that this notwithstanding, as a stone or corpse cannot perform any operation of which natural life is the principle, because they have it not; neither can a man in his fallen state put forth an act of spiritual life, because he is without that life and grace that is the principle thereof: For as the soul is to the body, with respect to natural life, so is the new nature to the soul, with respect to a moral, or spiritual life.

---

[1] In the original, Coxe does not proceed to a second response to Collier's reply above but continues with multiple sub-points.

That which he offers that he might escape the force of this testimony is so remote from the evident scope of the texts insisted on, that I shall not need to return any particular answer thereto, but leave his error crushed under the weight of these sayings of the Holy Ghost, who hath in them stained the pride of all flesh: Only I could wish that they into whose hands these lines may come, would also consult Dr. Owen in his Discourse of the Spirit, where he doth largely plead and vindicate these texts against the Pelagians, Arminians, &c. from whom Mr. Collier hath drank in these notions. For my own part, I had not now produced them, but only that I might take this opportunity to remove his objections against their true sense, supposing this a convenient place for that work; seeing my design is only to remove his cavils out of the way of weak Christians, and not to handle any point myself, farther than in the pursuit thereof I am led to: I pass therefore a multitude of other Scriptures that contradict his notion, and shall attend him, in his proof offered, and discover the weakness and insufficiency thereof.

The first thing which he saith proves his opinion is:

"*Because it is the duty of all men (suitable to the means and ministry they have been under) to believe and obey God.*" And after he hath by divers texts proved this, which none denies, he adds:

> "*All which proves a capacity in men to answer his will, or we must reflect on God,*" &c.

Were man to be considered in his primitive state, as he came out of the hands of God, there were some weight in this reasoning. But to suppose that the duty of man must be measured by his power and ability in his fallen state, is fond, and groundless: He cannot sin himself from under obligation to duty. Though he lose the image of God, that rectitude of nature, by his sin, that enabled him to obey God, yet the most high doth not lose his right of commanding him, that which is just and good. In truth, to say that we have power in and of ourselves, to do all that God requires of us, is in effect, to make void the grace of God, and to renounce the Gospel; at least to allow its usefulness (which is the most Mr. Collier doth) only to facilitate the discharge of our duty. But if our duty is to be measured by our power, it will appear that sinners hardened by continuance in sin, and profligate wickedness, are most excusable; seeing they have least power to obey God (as Mr. Collier will confess) and so by his argument it were unjust with God to require that of them, which he doth of others not immersed in their debaucheries. Yea let me add this also; from Dr. Owen pg. 245 of his pneuma,tolog (*sic*):

> In the transactions between God and the souls of men, with respect unto their obedience and salvation, there is none of them but hath a power in sundry things, as to some degrees and measures of them, to comply with his mind and will, which they voluntarily neglect; and this of itself is sufficient to bear the charge of their eternal ruin.[2]

The second thing whereby he endeavors to prove his opinion, pg. 25, is, "*Because God blames those under all his ministrations, that did not or do not suitably obey him therein:*" To which he adds in the third place, "*He threatens and executes judgment on all such.*"

Both these depend on the first; and no man besides Mr. Collier would have made use of them as distinct mediums in the proof of his position.

The first therefore being enervated, these fall with it. But he saith, if we accept not this as a sufficient proof of his notion, "*We cannot

---

[2] John Owen, *PNEUMATOLOGIA: or, A Discourse Concerning the Holy Spirit* (London: Nathaniel Ponder, 1674), 245.

have right, honorable, and God-like thoughts of the Lord, to require, blame, pity, promise, threaten, and execute terrible judgment on a people, that in no case was able to help it."

He that can make good sense of these words, hath more skill than I, but I heartily wish non-sense had been the worst fault in Mr. Collier's book, however it be, I will endeavor to give a distinct answer to that which he drives at.

1. God may require obedience of those from whom it is due, though they have sinned away their power to perform it.

2. It is a moral sinful impotency that men are under, they cannot, nor they will not obey, but they can and do willfully refuse to obey God, and therefore are justly blamed and punished for this wickedness, and are also as creatures, the objects of pity while they thus destroy themselves.

3. Promises and threatenings are fit mediums to work upon rational creatures, who are capable of understanding the terms in which the things of the Spirit of God are proposed to them (though the glory of the things themselves, they discern not) and to put forth a free act of their wills in reference to them; as Mr. Collier saith himself in his *Body of Divinity*, pg. 452, *"Though man hath lost the freedom of his will to that which is good by sinning, yet not the power of willing."* And

4. By the mighty power of God's Spirit giving efficacy to this means, the Elect are made obedient, and the rest left without excuse or cloak for their sin.

As for that clause, that *"in no case was able to help it,"* it is fallacious. They act spontaneously, and are in no case willing to help it, whose souls are not renewed by special grace. He goes on, pg. 26:

It must be so because the contrary leaves the condemnation of sinners at God's door, which far be it from any sober spirit to imagine: For God to bring forth a glorious ministration of grace and life to the world, 1 and tender it to sinners on such terms as is impossible for them to perform; with the help he affords, 2 and to damn them for non-performance thereof, necessarily leaves a necessity of perishing without hope or help. So that if this were true, that men could not believe and obey the Gospel, where it comes 3 simply from their debility and impotency, and the debility of the means afforded them for help therein; it could not be their sin. 4 For it is no man's sin, not to do what he cannot do, but what he can and might do had he a will to it.

The things before pleaded, do fully remove out of our way what is here offered: But farther to detect his equivocation; mind,

1. Although it be impossible for dead sinners to quicken themselves; yet seeing this impossibility is founded in the corruption of their natures, and wickedness of their own hearts, it cannot in the least excuse their disobedience.

2. Sinners are liable to damnation for the breach of the Law, and if they add hereunto disobedience to the Gospel, it necessarily aggravates their sin and condemnation; and this they will do, if left to themselves; but neither doth this necessity, which is only a necessity of infallibility, with respect to the event, in any wise infringe their liberty, or excuse their sin,

3. Whereas he talketh of unbelief that "*comes simply from the debility and impotency of men, and the debility of the means afforded them;*" and in the next section, "*Of that which befalls a man that, he could not, nor in any case cannot help,*" &c. I must tell him, that it is dishonestly done to represent this, as the opinion of the men with whom his controversy is; seeing they teach, that man's disobedience to God springs from their obstinacy, and not only

impotency; and they are condemned for that, and not simply for this alone, and also, that the means of salvation tendered in the Gospel, is full and gloriously perfect in its kind: But the reason why the Gospel is not effectual to the salvation of all that hear it is, the natural enmity and obstinacy of their hearts against God is such, that unless it be overcome and cured, by him that raised Christ from the dead, they do finally resist the call of God, and will not come to Christ that they might have life: And this defilement of human nature man brought upon himself by his fall, which he could have helped and prevented if he would, and it is approved and delighted in by all his posterity.

4. The falsehood therefore of his saying, "*That is no man's sin not to do what he cannot do,*" is evident, seeing man's duty is determined by God's holy command, not his own sinful weakness. So then our doctrine doth not lay the sin of men at God's door (as he suggests) but at their own, where the Scripture lays it; it spoileth man indeed of all matter of boasting, which is the true reason of Mr. Collier's endeavor to load it with this calumny.

And in truth though proud hypocrites will be boasting of their self-sufficiency, we need not nor can have a more pathetical confutation of Mr. Collier's doctrine, than that which is gathered from the confession of one poor in spirit, and distressed in soul, under the sense of his lost condition by nature. Methinks I see such an one rolling himself in the dust, and with floods of tears, and groanings that cannot be uttered, pouring out his soul before the Lord with such expressions as these:

> "O Lord look down in mercy upon a captivated condemned sinner, that hath broken thy holy Law, and finds nothing in himself but a principle of enmity to, and aversation from thy holy will revealed either in the Law or in the Gospel; I confess that it is a miracle of mercy,

that terms of pardon and acceptance by Jesus are proposed to me: But ah Lord! My blindness is such that I shall never find this way of life, if thou do not lead me, and the hardness of my heart such, that it will not bow, unless thou make me willing in the day of thy power! I hear Christ say 'Come;' but alas! I cannot come; oh draw my soul to thyself by thine effectual grace! Heaven is opened to the believer; but O Lord! That word believe slays my heart; it is my duty I confess, and ever to be admired is grace, that found out such a remedy: But oh my unbelief! I am shut up under it! What shall I do! Whither shall I flee! Lord faith is thy Gift, and by thine almighty power it hath been wrought in some such as I am: Oh magnify grace in me a lost creature, even me also! Renew my soul, change my heart, make me a believer, work in me both to will and to do of thy good pleasure, else I may as soon reach Heaven with my finger as believe; my impotency, my blindness, the perverseness of my heart is so great! I must confess O Lord thou art just if thou damn me; but oh pity! And save a soul without might, that is now sinking under thy wrath, if free, free grace prevent not, by working in me what thou requirest of me."

I return to Mr. Collier who will now give us instances to illustrate his former assertion, and (that he may take this opportunity, to let out more of his poisonous doctrine) chiefly insists on Original Sin, which he endeavors to persuade men is an harmless thing, and of itself lays them under no more guilt, than doth a fit of sickness, or any other affliction of the like kind, that no man can help, &c. Only thus much he grants,

"It's true the first death is come on all men by Adam's transgression, they having the same original nature of sin and

death, it is come into all men as a judgment for the first transgression, but not as a sin to the second death."

Although it may not be easy to find out any good sense of these words [the original nature of sin and death] yet it is easy to understand what is the drift of his discourse, which he also farther explains anon, and which I before touched: And therefore to prevent him, before I examine what he saith, I will briefly propose the truth concerning this point as it is taught in the Scriptures, Rom. 5 and other places, viz. Job 14.4; Psalm 51.5; John 3.6, &c., from whence I gather:

1. That Adam in his primitive state was to be considered as a public person, in whom all mankind (that in an ordinary way of generation came of him) were; and in whom they sinned and fell, when he fell: And they are to be considered in him legally and naturally:

    1. Legally as he was (according to the terms of the covenant in which he stood related to God) their representative; and so received his perfections, or original righteousness, for them as well as for himself, and they as well as he lost it by the fall.

    2. Naturally, as he was the root of all mankind, which were virtually in his loins when he fell. So then:

2. Original Sin is either imputed or inherent. The imputation of Adam's sin to his posterity, by which they are most justly accounted to have sinned in him, who was the root, and both generative and federal principle of mankind, is in some sort the meritorious cause of the inherent pravity of the human nature derived from him, which is diffused through all the parts of the soul, and is a just punishment for the first offense; by which we are turned away from God, and disposed to all

wickedness, it being the root, seed, and principle of all actual transgressions and sins; and is therefore so frequently by the Apostle Paul called sin in a way of emphasis; and the flesh; of which all the abominations that are in the world are the proper fruit and offspring, and are so represented by him, Rom. 7.8 &c.; 13.14; Gal. 5.19; Col. 2.11; Eph. 2.3.

3. When therefore we affirm with the Apostle, Rom. 5.18, that by the offense of one, judgment came upon all men unto condemnation; neither doth the Holy Ghost in that text, nor we, intend to assert, that any are actually damned for Adam's particular fact; but, that by his sin and our sinning in him, by God's most just ordination, we have lost original righteousness, and so (as darkness necessarily is, where light is taken away or denied, and sickness where health is not) contracted that exceeding pravity and sinfulness of nature, which deserveth the curse of God and eternal damnation; and it is inherent uncleanness that actually excludes out of the Kingdom of God.

From what hath been said, it is easy to gather how pernicious Mr. Collier's doctrine is, who teacheth, that Original Sin exposeth only to temporal or bodily, not eternal death. The Apostle constantly affirms, Rom. 5, that it is the death and condemnation, that Christ saveth his people from (which surely is the second, not the first death), which by our fall in Adam we were exposed to, and guilty of.

But why doth not Original Sin deserve the second death? Is it because Adam's transgression was but trivial, certainly the aggravations of his sin were exceeding great: There was contempt of God, disbelief of his word, pride, breach of covenant, theft, murder &c. all combined in that one sin; so that a greater (the sin against the Holy Ghost excepted) and more complex evil, none of the sons of men were ever guilty of. But if this had not been, there is no sin in its own nature so final, but *ratione objecti* [3] in that it is against an infinite majesty, it deserves everlasting punishment; as every one that fears God, and knows his terror can tell. Is it because the corruption of our nature derived from Adam is but a small thing? Who trembles not at such a thought, that hath not cast off all sense of a deity, and the holiness thereof? We have before proved, that it is the spring of all the evil that is done under the sun; it is in its own nature a principle of enmity to God, that from whence the heart of man is denominated to be deceitful above all things, and desperately wicked.

If there be anything therefore in what he saith besides his bold affirmation, it is only this:

> *"Because it is a judgment for the first transgression, it cannot be a sin to the second death."*

But he may learn from the Scriptures, that God oft-times punisheth sinners by giving them up to sin, and yet that sin, which hath also in it a punishment of former transgression, will sink a soul under divine wrath, as well as any other. Let him take for instance, Rom. 1.21; *ad finem*;[4] 2 Thess. 2.10-12.

I thought in my reply to this, and what followeth, to have shown how Mr. Collier in some things takes the Pelagian notion of Original Sin, in effect plainly enough denying it; and also how in asserting the defilement of our nature, not to be our sin, he agrees with Bellarmine[5] and other Jesuits, in their opposition to the Protestant doctrine in this point. But I must be brief; and shall therefore content myself only to show his repugnancy to the truth of God in the Scripture. Thus he goes on:

---

[3] *"By virtue of the fact that...."*
[4] *"To the end."*
[5] Roman Cardinal Robert Bellarmine (1542-1621), one of the most erudite opponents of the Reformed faith. See F.L. Cross and E.A. Livingstone, eds. *The Oxford Dictionary of the Christian Church* (Oxford: OUP, 1997), 181.

> *"All men are born into the world with sinful natures, now this defilement of our natures (though sinful) no man can help; therefore it is not their sin, but their affliction."*

Here is a sinful nature, a sinful defilement of nature; and yet no sin but an affliction only! Let such confusion be the lot of all that oppose God's sacred truth! Can the nature of man be defiled, and sinful, and yet he not a sinner? Yea but *"... no man can help it, therefore it is not their sin."* I answer:

This defilement of human nature came by that sin, that man might not have committed; he might have helped it if he would. Yea moreover Original Sin, is habitually in the will as the subject thereof as well as other faculties of the soul, and therefore is voluntary; and every particular person is to be accounted, and truly is, the immediate principle as well as the subject, the author as well as the possessor, of his own individual Original Sin, or corruption of nature, even as a man is of his natural faculties, or acquired habits, or as Adam himself was of this Original Sickness or Disease, in his own person: as the learned Voetius asserts in his short book of *Select Disputations*, pg. 1105.[6]

And it is by reason of this defilement of nature, that we are "**by nature the children of wrath;**" which could not be, if it were not our sin, Eph. 2.3. And on this ground the Lord Christ asserts the necessity of regeneration, and that without it none can see the Kingdom of God, John 3.5-7. Mr. Collier saith farther,

> *And cause we have to bewail it as our affliction; but not as our sin; so the Apostle doth, Rom. 7.24. It is consenting to it which is the sin, v. 15-16; James 1.14-15, when persons consent to covetous and worldly lusts, to proud, envious, and disobedient lusts; this is the sin that will usher in the second*

---

[6] Gisberti Voetii, *Selectarum Disputationum Pars Quinta* (Ultrajecti: Antonii Smytegelt, 1669). Gisbertus Voetius (1589-1676) was a highly respected Dutch Reformed theologian. See Cross and Livingstone, *Oxford Dictionary*, 1706.

death: Original guilt and stain only brings under the first death, but not the second as distinct from consent.

Original Sin may be considered either in the unregenerate in whom it reigns, and is wholly unmortified; or as remaining in the regenerate, though mortified and spoiled of its reigning power. The unregenerate are under the power thereof in all the faculties of their souls. It is blindness and vanity in their minds; hatred of God, and obstinacy in their wills, &c. and they are content to be commanded by this principle, and the first moral acting of the soul is influenced thereby, Psalm 58.3, and in them the lustings of the flesh are never resisted, from any true hatred of their sinfulness, though on other accounts, as they are apprehended destructive to themselves one way or other, they may be so, in some particular actings thereof. But in the regenerate there is a contrary principle, even the Law of the Spirit of Life which is in Christ Jesus that sets them free from the Law of sin and death, so that they obey not the flesh in the lusts thereof; and these, as they are by the power of the Spirit of Grace delivered from the service of sin, so are they also by the efficacy of Christ's blood saved from the condemning power thereof. "**There is no condemnation to them**," Rom. 8.1. But it is not because indwelling sin deserves none, but because "**Jesus saveth them from the wrath to come**." Now such an one is personated by Paul, Rom. 7, unto whom all sin is an afflicting burden; and the lustings of indwelling sin, which were opposed by the new creature, he complains of as his greatest affliction, but not as his affliction only, as outward trouble and persecution was, but as his sin also: Nay therefore it was his affliction, because his sin, and so he calls it about ten times in that chapter, and as such bitterly bewails it. Let the text be consulted for proof hereof. "**In me**," saith he, "**that is in my flesh** (in me so far as not renewed by grace) **dwells no good thing:**" Now sin is ἀνομία,[7] a privation of that good and holiness that the Law requires, and this saith the

---

[7] "*Lawlessness.*"

Apostle is in me: and yet Mr. Collier supposeth he acknowledgeth no sin; but this may be in a rational creature, and he not a sinner. Yea the Apostle confesseth, that he was greatly hindered in his duty by the working of his corruption, and at last flies to Christ for deliverance therefrom, and yet shall we say he owneth no fault all this while?

As for James 1.14-15, the evident scope of the Apostle is, not to teach men to justify the wicked lustings of their hearts, as Mr. Collier doth; but to prove that the spring of all the wickedness of man, is in his own breast, and it will be in vain for him to think of shifting off the blame to any other. It is granted indeed, that the Apostle saith, "**Lust when it hath conceived bringeth forth sin**;" and that this conceiving of sin is by the consent of the will, agreeing to the commission thereof; but by sin here, it is evident that actual transgression is intended; and what saith the Apostle of this lust? Verily, that it tempteth, draweth away the soul from God, and enticeth it to sin; and that it worketh thus as a principle in the soul, it is a man's "own lust." Shall we then suppose actual transgression to be a sin, and the working of that principle in a man that disposeth to it, not to be so? Hath God no regard to the hearts and principles of men, and the habits of their souls? Do not they come under his Law? Or is not the habit of grace, grace as well as the exercise thereof, and a man denominated gracious therefrom? And here *oppositorum par ratio*,[8] in plain terms; to suppose the lustings of a corrupt heart after all wickedness, is no harm, unless they be fully consented to, is impious.

As to that which he adds concerning infants and idiots; to suppose them no way concerned in sin as he doth, and so well enough without Christ, is like the rest of his doctrine: This I say, because the Scripture saith it, which declares all to be under sin (even those that have not sinned after the similitude of Adam's transgression, viz. actually) and all sin to deserve wrath; that neither infants nor idiots can stand before God without a mediator: They have sin enough to

---

[8] Loosely, "*a reason or argument being a counterpart or equal to its opposites.*" In other words, employing the same argument in reverse.

damn them, but there is grace enough in God, and merit enough in the blood of Christ to save them, unto which (and not their own innocency) they must be beholding for salvation.

The 5th thing he insists on to prove his opinion, is God's expostulating with men to convince them of the equality of his ways: That the ways of God towards the sons of men are full of equity and grace, is evident from what I have already proved in opposition to his errors; and to his harangue about it, I shall only say: There is no need for him to speak wickedly for God: His righteousness is abundantly manifested by the light of Scripture doctrine, without the help of his notions, and shall be yet farther manifested in the day of Christ, to the shame and silencing of all that now reply against God, even in those things where his judgments are a great deep: As the Apostle discourseth at large Rom. 9 and 11 chapters.

The objection that he starts about God his creating man upright, &c. I need not long stay upon; the truth concerning this is before stated and proved; and every impartial reader may see, how miserably he trifles in his endeavor to solve it: He gives you his word for it, that God will excuse men from all that obedience that they have by their sin lost both power and will to perform. But I hope none are so credulous as to take his book to be canonical. Not one text of Scripture doth he, nor can he produce for the proof of his opinion; but only attempts to back one falsehood with another, saying that:

> *"Since the fall God requireth not perfect obedience of men, but only sincerity, and that he knew that man might yield sincere obedience in faith and love, and in that hath promised both assistance, and acceptance in his Son,"* &c.

Two things he here takes for granted, but both without ground.

1. That all the world are under the Covenant of Grace, so as to be presently interested in the privileges thereof, and accepted in those sincere endeavors to obey God, which they are

capable of in that condition wherein they are by nature, which is not so; For all that can be said of men in general unto whom the Gospel is preached, amounts to no more than this, that the grace and blessings of the New Covenant are offered to them upon condition of faith: God declareth his good pleasure to sinners, that if they or any of them do confess and forsake their sins, "**they shall find mercy**;" and those of them that do believe, he gives the sure mercies of David unto, Isa. 55.3, and they are under Grace, Rom. 6.14. But the rest of the world are under the severity of the Law still, yea whosoever doth in heart depart from Christ, and seek life by his own works, is a debtor to answer the most rigorous demands thereof, and is fallen from grace, Christ shall profit him nothing, Gal. 5.3-4. And that passage 2 Cor. 8.12, "**For if there be first a willing mind, it is accepted according to what a man hath, and not according to what he hath not:**" is pitifully wrested by Mr. Collier in that he would apply it to the case in hand: for neither the thing nor persons there spoken of, will at all agree thereto.

1. It is not a moral sinful impotency or deficiency, that the Apostle there speaks of: But only a want of riches, and ability in that respect to contribute so largely to the necessity of the poor saints, as otherwise they might and would have done.

2. The persons spoken of are saints, believers, such as are accepted in Christ, and interested in the Covenant of Grace; whose sincere endeavors to walk with God, are according to the terms of that covenant accepted by him through the beloved (though this obedience of theirs is not their justifying righteousness, nor accepted for that end). But the case is otherwise with persons out of Christ.

Mr. Collier endeavors to strengthen this notion, pg. 32, by proving, that "*Under Moses Law, sincerity was accepted, and that though the Law required perfect obedience, yet this perfection consisted, in universality and sincerity,*" &c.

But here again he pitifully confounds things that ought to be heedfully distinguished.

In the Mosaical economy, there was such a remembrance of the Covenant of Works revived, with the terms and sanction thereof; as that hereupon it is called the ministration of condemnation, and did engender unto bondage, 2 Cor. 3.7; Gal. 4.25. But yet the promise of salvation by the Messiah, being made long before, was not enervated thereby; but even this was laid in a subserviency to Gospel ends; and also the Gospel was preached to them, Heb. 4.2 (and so the Covenant of Grace revealed) though more darkly in types and shadows, through which they were instructed, to seek Justification unto Life by Christ promised, and so deliverance from the curse of the Law by him. Now amongst these some did believe, others did not; and so some were related to God in the New Covenant, others remained under the Old: The sincere obedience of the one was accepted on Gospel gracious terms, and for Gospel ends (not that they obtained life thereby, according to the terms of the Covenant of Works, "**Do this and live**") Christ being their surety to answer the utmost demands of the Law, for their Justification before God. The other were in their own persons responsible for the breach of the Law, and stood guilty of death by the curse thereof, as well for want of absolute perfection, as sincerity in their obedience, for the Covenant of Works considered formally as such, knows no change of sincerity for perfection, but its commands must in every respect be obeyed, and its demands answered, and they are so by Christ alone who hath fulfilled the righteousness thereof for them that do believe; and without faith in him, the soul stands or falls to the unallayed and most rigorous sentence thereof.

[2.]⁹ The second thing Mr. Collier supposeth is:

"That every man hath ability in his fallen state to yield sincere obedience to God in faith and love."

This hath been already refuted, and here is nothing offered to inforce it, I shall therefore refer the reader to that which precedes in this chapter: Where also the foundation of what Mr. Collier farther pleads in his two following sections, is fully removed, so that there remains only a flourish of words, wherewith he beats the air; in returning answer to which, I shall waste no more precious time.

---

⁹ This is not in the original but has been added for clarity.

CHAPTER V

Wherein Some Things Relating to the Principles Already Asserted, Are Farther Cleared and Vindicated: And Also The Saints Perseverance Proved, and Thomas Collier's Exceptions Removed.

I am now come to his fifth chapter, wherein he endeavors farther to strengthen his opinions before laid down, and is more express in his asserting believers final falling away from grace: The most of what he saith is built on those principles that have been already discussed; and therefore in my examination thereof, I will only note, either those things which are very gross, or that wherein he seems to offer something that hath not before been urged and answered.

Those texts which he endeavors to wrest in the beginning of this chapter, have been already vindicated from his corrupt glosses, I do therefore here pass them over, and attend to what he saith, pg. 31, where he propounds this question:

> *"May we suppose that persons may believe, or that any do believe unto life, only by the objective evidence, or external ministry, without the Spirit's work in and with the Gospel?"* His answer is, *"If we may suppose the ministry to go without the Spirit working therein, then we may suppose a possibility in respect of power, else men could not be condemned for not believing,"* &c.

The absurd folly of his supposition, *"That by our sin we cut God short of right to command our obedience to his holy will, as well as lose our power to obey,"* hath been already detected: By this and what followeth, you may see (what I said before) that this man doth not stick at the grossest Pelagianism, but supposeth man in his fallen state, by his corrupt mind and natural capacity, without any work of God's Spirit upon him, to be capable of discerning, believing, and yielding acceptable obedience to the revelations of God contained in the Scriptures of truth. Howbeit we have heard the Scripture teacheth other doctrine: And the Apostle Paul was so far from this proud conceit of himself, that he confesseth the quite contrary, viz. 2 Cor. 3.5, **"That we are not sufficient of ourselves to think anything as of ourselves, but our sufficiency is of God,"** i.e. It is of God in a way of grace, who works all our works in us. But against the saying of the Apostle, he excepts pg. 43:

> *"It's true as of ourselves only we are not, distinct from Christ and Gospel grace we are not; but by the helps afforded there is power both to will and to do the will of God in the Gospel."*

It seems by these words of Thomas Collier, that he is conscious to himself that this text doth overthrow his notion of the sufficiency of men without any help of the Spirit of God to do anything that is truly and spiritually good, especially those that are utter strangers to Christ, and Gospel grace; for he now owns that distinct from Christ and Gospel grace we have no such sufficiency: But he doth not use to trouble himself, to keep an harmony in his book, betwixt pages so far distant as is page 31 from 43, and therefore it is no marvel to find him here unsaying what before he said; and instead of that, to content himself for the present with asserting, that "*There is a sufficient help afforded to all,*" &c. But brings forth no proof of that neither; but besides what hath been already proved against him, I shall farther examine this notion, before I come to the end of this chapter; and at present manifest, that it is overthrown by this text: The Apostle doth in these words (not with a feigned modesty) but from his heart confess he is beholding to the grace of God, for every good thing wrought in him or by him; and therefore he instanceth in that which scarce amounts to any good work, even a thought; when he affirmeth our sufficiency to be of God, and denyeth that we are ἱκανοι[1] *sufficient* or *meet* for it; any way capable of ourselves to exert, or frame a good thought in our own breasts: And this he denies of himself when converted, and refers all the praise of the exercise of grace in his soul to the Spirit of God even then; now it is less to think than to will, and less to, will than to perform: And if our ability for the former be denied, it must be so much more for the latter: And if it be denied of a converted man, much more of one unconverted: It is repugnant to reason and Scripture evidence to think, that the blessed Apostle, a person in all respects qualified with natural endowments and education, yea in an eminent manner assisted by the Spirit of God, should say that he had no sufficiency of his own, for anything that was truly good, and in the meanwhile to suppose that any unconverted person, hath power of himself to be so good, in thought, will, and deed, as to get to Heaven by the mere improvement of his natural capacity, without any assistance of divine grace.

In pg. 32 he farther opens his mind about conversion, and tells us, "*If God did not work at all by his Spirit, but only give the Gospel which hath in itself a natural tendency to draw sinners to Christ, if according to their capacities they believe and obey it, they should undoubtedly be saved.*"

---

[1] The original reads ἰχανοι.

There are two things supposed in these words, the one true, the other utterly untrue; a common artifice of deceivers to make their notions pass the more readily with the weak that cannot discover their imposture herein.

1. He supposeth that whosoever believeth and obeyeth the Gospel by any means, is under the promise of salvation, which is a great truth; these two, viz. faith and salvation being inseparably connected in the Scripture.

2. He takes it for granted (as before) that a man in his natural estate, without any the least assistance from the Spirit of God, hath a sufficient ability, and is in a capacity to believe and obey the Gospel; And so all that he allows to the Spirit of God, is but to render the work of conversion the more facile and easy, for thus he writes again pg. 33, that "*After believing and obeying the Gospel, God usually gives a greater measure of his Spirit; so that after believing, Christians are or might be, in a better capacity to live to God than before.*" They were therefore in a capacity to live to God before believing; and again pg. 34:

    "*As the Apostle speaks in the matter of prayer, Rom. 8.26, He helpeth our infirmities, so it is true in all cases; the work of the Spirit is to help our infirmities, for it is we that do believe and obey the Gospel, and not the Spirit.*" The result or necessary consequence of these words of his is, that persons may believe and never be beholding to the Spirit; they *can convert themselves* without him: But if he do *ex abundanti*[2] afford his help, it is not to convert the soul by his own power and grace, but only to facilitate the work, by exciting a principle that he finds in the soul, and which was there before any special working of his in and upon it.

---

[2] "*Out of his abundance.*"

But if we consult the holy Scriptures, we shall find that in them conversion is spoken of in a dialect far differing from Mr. Collier's. For instance James 1.18, "**Of his own will hath he begotten us**," &c. Now this new birth, or being begotten of God, doth bespeak plainly the infusing of that gracious principle into the soul that was not there before; and this is done by the Spirit of God, in the exercise of sovereign grace. "**As the wind bloweth where it listeth, so of his own will hath he begotten us.**" Of the same import is that phrase, of "**taking the heart of stone out of the flesh, and giving an heart of flesh; a new heart,**" so often mentioned in the Covenant of Grace, and can signify no less than the effectual removing and curing of that wicked disposition of soul, and stubbornness of heart, by which a person is kept in rebellion against God, by communicating to them a divine nature, as it is called 2 Pet. 1.4. So also conversion is called a "**new creation**," and grace the "**new man**," or a "**new creature**," 2 Cor. 5.17; Eph. 4.24; 2.10, which terms in the common sense of men, signify the production of that which before was not in being, by a divine power, even the same that wrought in Christ, when he was raised from the dead, Eph. 1.19-20, and do not suppose any predisposition or inclination in the person where this new creation is not, exciting the great Creator to a concurrence or assistance in order to its production. Yet Mr. Collier hath the boldness to say, that all these expressions amount to no more (if rightly weighed) than what he hath asserted, viz. that "*God doth help men to believe, by the working of his Spirit with them; so cherishing the good he finds in them that it be not mastered by the sensual brutish part.*" Greater contempt hath not lightly been cast upon the Holy Spirit of God, who works all grace in us; nor upon his sayings in the Scripture, whereby his operation on the souls of men is unfolded to us; as if the Holy Ghost intended to persuade them, that they are beholding to distinguishing grace for that, which in truth they have in nature, and do themselves.

The reason that Mr. Collier gives for his talking at this rate, is, "*Because it is we that believe and obey the Gospel, and not the Spirit: And it is our duty, and so stated in the Scripture.*"

By this he intends to prove, that the Spirit of God is not the only and principal efficient cause of faith in men; but they open their own eyes, and raise themselves from the dead, and create themselves anew in Christ Jesus; or else believing must be attributed to the Spirit, and not to them, and must be considered as his duty, and not theirs.

I might tell Mr. Collier (seeing he pretends to learning) *Qui actionis causa efficiens principalis & prima est; non illico ab actione, cujus causa est denominatur (licet in illam per modum causae particularis determinantis influat) sed ille tantum qui actione informatur.*[3] But it is in vain to trouble his head with any philosophical notion: I shall rather make evident his mistake, by some familiar instance that may be within his reach. And I know none fitter to the case in hand, than that of Lazarus his resurrection from the dead by Christ. I suppose it will be granted that the Lord did not only help Lazarus to live and come out of his grave, but that by his divine power he made him to live, that was before dead and utterly uncapable of action; yet was it Lazarus that came forth, and revived, not Christ. So though the Spirit of God do give life to the soul, and by his own power make it to believe, yet is it the man converted, not the Spirit that believes, &c.

To make the matter more plain we must remember, that there are two moments in conversion to be considered. The first is the infusion of a principle of life and grace, by which the soul is enabled and disposed to convert and believe, being renewed after the image of God; and this is called *gratia prima*,[4] the "first grace," in the reception whereof we are passive. The second is, the exercise of this grace in actual turning to God, believing, &c. through the blessed assistance of the Good Spirit, who worketh in us to do as well as to will; and this is called *gratia secunda*.[5] In this the soul is active, and works according to the working of him who works in it mightily.

---

[3] "*He who is the efficient cause of an act is principal [or] original and first; he is named [such] not because of the act of which he is the cause (although he flows into that [act] through the mode of the particular determining cause) but only to such a degree as the one who is formed by the action.*"
[4] "First grace."
[5] "Second grace."

Before I pass farther, I think it may be a convenient place here to remove out of our way, the corrupt glosses of Mr. Collier upon a text or two, which he is pleased to take notice of towards the end of this chapter.

The first is John 15.5, mentioned by him pg. 39. The words are, **"Without me ye can do nothing."** The design of Christ in these words, is to press his disciples to abide in him; for this end he tells them in this verse, **"I am the vine, ye are the branches; he that abideth in me and I in him, the same bringeth forth much fruit; for without me** (or, severed from me χωρὶς ἐμοῦ[6]) **ye can do nothing."**

We are by nature dry branches, and unfruitful, meet fuel for the fire of God's wrath; and if ever we bring forth fruit to God, we must first by the powerful grace of God the great husband-man, be engrafted into Christ the true vine; that we may derive life and grace from him: neither will our admission into the Church suffice thereunto, without real union with himself, and cleaving to him by faith lively and unfeigned, by the daily exercise whereof we fetch new supplies of grace, so drawing sap, from him, from whom our fruit is found: Thus is he unto us as the vine unto the branches; for without Christ, i.e. the influence of his aid and grace, or in a state of separation, in which we are not capable of this vital influence from him, we can do nothing; understand it according to the subject matter, nothing that is spiritually good. Surely this casts man down from that throne of self-sufficiency, unto which Mr. Collier would advance him; and very poorly doth he acquit himself in his reply thereto; He saith:

> 1. *"All the common light, understanding and reason that men have is from him."*

This is the refuge of the Pelagians of old, in which Mr. Collier hath before attempted to shelter himself: They would pretend to own

---

[6] *"Apart from me."*

the grace of God, when their meaning was no more than this, that men as men, were beholden to God for their natural accomplishments; more than which they neither had, nor needed from him, to enable them to yield acceptable obedience to him: But that something else is intended in this text, we have already manifested.

> 2. *"The Gospel leads souls to him, where their help is; it is that which I say there is no capacity or power without the Gospel, which unites souls to Christ in whom their life is,"* &c.

It is the faith of the Gospel, and not the bare hearing of it that unites the soul to Christ; and though Mr. Collier here tell us of drawing to Christ, and union with him, &c. yet his design is still to exclude the special and effectual work of the Spirit, to bring the soul to Christ, and preserve it in him, which I before proved necessary hereunto. And there is little heed to be taken to his saying, *"There is no power or capacity without the Gospel:"* This is but to serve a present turn; for he hath in his foregoing chapters pleaded, that *"Where the Gospel never comes, men have sufficient means and power to live to God without it."*

The second text is 1 Cor. 4.7, **"Who maketh thee to differ, and what hast thou, that thou hast not received?"** So Mr. Collier reads it, pg. 43, about which we need not contend: Add thereunto the close of the verse, **"Now if thou didst receive it, why dost thou glory as if thou hadst not received it?"** From hence we may safely infer, that if any man differ from another, or from what he was in himself before; that is to say, be raised from a state of death in sins and trespasses, unto newness of life; delivered from the power of darkness, and translated into the kingdom of the Son of God's love; it is God hath made this difference, to the praise of the riches of his grace. And thus much Mr. Collier in answer to the objection grants, *"It is God by Gospel grace makes us to differ."* But if Mr. Collier's notion elsewhere be true, that *"Amongst men that receive every way as much grace from God the one as the other, some believe unto life, others remain in their sins;"* it will necessarily follow, that those of them which choose the better part, do make themselves to differ, and have cause of boasting, if not before God, yet in comparison with other men. And this is in terms denied by the Apostle; and Mr. Collier makes no reply thereto, but what hath now been oft mentioned and answered; and therefore I will not trouble the reader with a repetition of it.

The text that remains to be insisted on, is Phil. 2.13, "**For it is God which worketh in you, both to will and to do, of his good pleasure.**" That this Scripture is directly opposite to Mr. Collier's doctrine, is evident. In the foregoing verse he exhorts the Philippians to "work out their own salvation with fear and trembling." By "**working out their salvation**," he intends laboring for, or bestowing their utmost industry to obtain salvation; and according to this sense is the same word rendered, John 6.27, "**Labor not for the meat that perisheth**," &c. Now hereunto two things are required:[7]

1. A principle enabling and disposing them to walk humbly with God in faith and obedience.

2. The exercise thereof, which is referred unto the internal acts of the will, and external operations in duties suitable thereunto.

And as we have before proved, that grace is wrought in us by the Spirit of God, so the Apostle here expressly affirms, that both to will and to do (which expressions take in the whole of its exercise) is also effectually wrought in us by him, "**of his own good pleasure**;" which is the most prevailing argument and motive to an humble walking with God, and encouragement thereto.

He that reads Mr. Collier's gloss upon this text, pg. 43, will find

---

[7] In the margin: "Dr. O's pneum. pg. 496," referring to John Owen's *PNEUMATOLOGIA*.

him constrained almost to embrace that notion of it that doth evert his opinion; and all that he offers towards the salving of it, is in these words, "*To understand it to intend God's working an impulsive will, and that they could not, or should not work without it, destroys the exhortation, and makes null the duty.*"

What Mr. Collier intends by an "*impulsive will*," or whether there be any good sense in those terms we need not inquire. That God worketh in us to will, or the very act of willing, the text is express: And it hath been already manifested to be his great error to conceive, that nothing is required of us in a way of duty, but what in our lapsed state we are able to perform without the help of God's Spirit. And therefore it is fallaciously done of him, to join those terms together, as if they were of equal extent; that they could not, or should not work without it: It was their indispensable duty to obey the exhortation foregoing; but this they could not do without the effectual working of God in them. And there is not more frequent mention of any one thing in the Gospel (it being that wherein Gospel grace doth eminently shine forth) than of our receiving grace from God to enable us to yield to him that obedience which he requires of us. Pious therefore and well-grounded was the petition of that worthy opposer of the Pelagians of old: *Da Domine quod jubes;* and *jube quod vis*:[8] "Give me O Lord what thou requirest of me, and command what thou pleasest." Indeed to deny that we receive anything from God in a way of special and distinguishing grace, that is required of us in a way of duty, is flatly to reject the Gospel, and to deny the grace of the New Covenant. We do not then destroy the exhortation, and make null the duty; but instruct men which way they may expect, and receive grace to obey it in the performance of their duty; which is certainly a great quickening and encouragement thereto, unto all that have an humble sense of their concernment in these things.

---

[8] The famous words of Augustine, "*Lord, give what you command; command what you will.*" See Philip Schaff, ed., Nicene and Post-Nicene Fathers (Peabody: Hendrickson, 2004 reprint), I:153.

I shall now return to Mr. Collier, pg. 34, where he propounds another question.

> "*Does the Spirit in the Gospel where it comes work in all alike? Or may we suppose that he effects a more special work in some than in others?*"

In answer hereunto he first tells us, that "*This is a mystery known only to God*;" and then immediately proceeds to give an account of very different operations of the Holy Ghost upon the children of men, as:

> 1. "*Some are convinced but not converted.*"

> 2. "*Others are wrought so far by the same Word and Spirit, as to believe and obey the Gospel so, as if they continue therein they shall be saved, Col. 1.21-23; 1 Tim. 2.15; Matt. 10.22.*"

> 3. "*Though the work be sufficient by which all might obtain the end, yet he worketh differingly, and giveth differing measures, for differing ends,*" &c.

> 4. "*His work on the special Elect is certain, and shall not leave them until it bring them to Glory.*"

Here we have another instance of the man's contradiction to himself; as well as unto truth. But to these things I say,

It is indeed certain from the Scriptures, that many are convinced, who never are converted by the Spirit of God, and also that the convictions of some proceed so far, as that they escape the pollutions that are in the world through lust, 2 Pet. 2.20, pass under that work described Heb. 6.4-6, and yet fail of those things that accompany salvation, which are things better than all that was before mentioned. Such with respect to their profession and general assent to the truth of the Gospel, &c. are said to believe for a time. And perseverance being the great touchstone of sincerity, the interest of persons in Christ, is oft referred thereto, with respect to the manifestation and proof thereof: So in Heb. 3.6 and those texts cited by Mr. Collier. If persons hold fast their rejoicing of hope, and confidence steadfast unto the end, it is evident they were sincere, and that their faith was of the right kind, in that it proves victorious against all opposition made thereto. But if they draw back, and fall away, their hypocrisy is detected, and it is made manifest that they were not of us; For if they had been of us no doubt they should have continued with us, 1 John 2.19. But the Scripture nowhere saith (as Mr. Collier supposeth) that these are in a saved condition, and heirs of glory, before their rottenness at heart is discovered; or that any sincere sound believer ever did, or ever shall return from life to death, from a state of redemption by Christ, and reconciliation unto God, into a state of bondage and enmity against God; from a state of Justification before God into a state of condemnation and wrath.

The Scripture also fully declares, that there are some who are "**the called according to God's purpose;**" a remnant according to the election of grace, that obtain like precious faith, through the effectual and saving operation of the Holy Ghost, who dwells in them, and by whose indwelling they are made lively members of Christ's mystical body, espoused to him and one spirit with him; but that any other than the Elect of God, predestinate to be conformed to the Image of his Son, called by his grace to the obedience of faith, are, or ever were in a state of salvation; the Scripture nowhere teacheth but the contrary. Those that are not vessels of mercy, are vessels of wrath. And that fiction of his, pg. 23, that "*The Spirit worketh in all Gospel believers (as he calls them) alike, which are the Elect in the threefold sense minded by him, which might all obtain, were they sincere, and constant to the end*;" is in this 35th page in part refuted by himself whilst he tells us, that "*The work of the Spirit on the special Elect is certain, and infallibly brings them to glory, but on others, some do wholly resist it, others though for a time they savingly comply with it, yet at last undo all* *again and destroy it.*" Certainly then here is a peculiar work of the Spirit, to be allowed in, and upon the special Elect, which in Scripture phrase are the only Elect unto salvation. Yet he supposeth that others are savingly wrought upon besides them, and some of these persevere, others fall away; and that many more are convinced, and all have a sufficient work, so as they might obtain the end, even those who notwithstanding never believe, nor are converted to God. And probably the thing he drives at in this question is, whether God doth more for, and the Spirit worketh more powerfully in one of these than the other. And first he pretends that this is a great secret, and God only knows it, but according to his principles it is easily resolved in the negative: For although (as the Arminians say) God draws some *modo congruo,* and others *modo non congruo*.[9] So that some have external and circumstantial advantages beyond others; yet there is no specific difference in the drawing itself; both the one and the other is only by way of moral suasion,[10] not physical operation, objective and external, not subjective and internal; and the turning cast still lies on the will of man, not the efficacy of grace. And I marvel that he should pretend so much modesty in this point, who but a little before hath asserted, that which all sober Arminians protest against, viz. the sufficiency or ability of man to believe, without any help from the Holy Ghost.

We have now met with Mr. Collier's assertion, that "*There is a sufficient work of the Spirit upon all, so that they might obtain the end;*" repeated *ad nauseam usq*:[11] It may not be amiss therefore to look into it a little more strictly. I say then:

1. Upon whomsoever the Spirit works in any degree, it is more than they deserve, it is of grace and not of debt, he is no way obliged to do so much for them; and even the common workings of the Spirit have in their own nature a tendency towards a farther good in the conversion of the soul, were they

---

[9] "*In a fitting manner;*" "*not in a fitting manner.*"
[10] I.e. "*persuasion.*"
[11] "*Ad nauseam everywhere.*"

not opposed and stifled by the enmity that is in man's heart unto God. But:

2. (To pass over many other things that might be urged) If the work of the Spirit upon all men be sufficient to bring them to Heaven, how cometh it to pass that all men are not saved? It will be answered, because many refuse to comply with, and resist his working upon, and striving with them. Be it so. I ask again, from whence ariseth his opposition to the Spirit of God, and his work in the souls of men? Certainly from that corruption of nature, and aversion of will from God, wherein all men are immersed by the Fall. But then the question returns on the other hand, how comes it to pass that all men do not perish in their obstinacy? The true answer is, because God prevents a remnant with distinguishing mercy, and quickens them whom he found dead in trespasses and sins (by his grace they are saved) and takes the heart of stone out of their flesh, and gives them an heart of flesh; thus making them a willing people in the day of his power; and considering man in that fallen condition wherein he is, there is no other work, of the Spirit sufficient to bring a lost sinner to grace and glory, but that by which his natural enmity to God is cured, and so the opposition of his soul to the work of the Holy Ghost overcome; even that work by which the heart is circumcised, and made willing and obedient that before was not so. And this Mr. Collier seems to own as the privilege of the special Elect; and without this none ever was, or will be converted.

In pg. 35, Mr. Collier proposeth a question about the foreknowledge of God, which he supposeth to be really distinct from his Decree; and though he be very unmeet to dispute such a question, yet he resolves to give the poor Calvinists another lash, before he finish his answer to it: Both question and answer are too confused for us to get any good by a particular examination of them; and therefore instead thereof, I will only give a brief account of what I understand in this matter, and so obviate his design.

The divine knowledge is variously distinguished, according to its respecting different objects; I shall at present consider it only as it is conversant about, things merely possible, or things future: Things only possible, are indifferent (considered as such) unto being or not being; and are such as in their own nature imply no contradiction unto being; even all things that fall within the unlimited compass of divine omnipotence: God knoweth all things that himself can do, though an infinite number of these never are done. Things future are all those things, and only those, which do in time come to pass. Now whatsoever hath, doth, or shall come to pass in time, was future from eternity; i.e. It was true from eternity that such things would be, and as things that would be were they known unto God before time. Seeing then some somethings were to be, and many things possible never shall be; it appears that some things were from eternity passed from the condition of things merely possible in which they were equally with others, by their own nature, into a condition of futurition: And there can be no cause aligned of this migration or passage, without God, for there was nothing before time but himself. It remains therefore that the cause thereof was in God; and indeed it was the will, purpose, or Decree of God, that some things should be, others should not, that alone made this change. So that the foreknowledge of things to be that is in God, supposeth his Decree that they shall be; and in truth, the foreknowledge or Decree of God, considered as in him, is the same; and the Scripture indifferently useth either term to denote the same thing; though we, because of the imbecility of our understanding, form differing conceptions of them, we conceive of the Decree as an act of God, willing that such things should be; and of divine prescience as an act of God, foreseeing or knowing the coming to pass of the things willed by him.

Amongst things future, some are good, some are evil, viz. morally. Those that are good God decreed to effect, those that are evil, to permit, or suffer to be done, knowing how, and having purposed in himself to order them, and overrule the doing of them for his own glory in the end. Again, some things we see, are the effects of causes that work necessarily, *necessitate consequentis*;[12] others of free agents, which are to us wholly contingent; yet do also necessarily come to pass, *necessitate consequentiae*.[13] And things are therefore thus effected in time, because God had decreed this order before time. Hence is the certainty of God's foreknowledge (which dependeth not on anything without himself) and so a necessity as to the event, that whatsoever hath been or shall be, should so come to pass as it doth: But this is a necessity of *infallibility*, not of *coaction*, and doth establish, not infringe the liberty of free agents.

I shall briefly apply these things to the case in hand: It will be granted I suppose, that the utmost end intended by God in all that comes to pass, is his own glory: He hath made all things for himself; and in the making of man, God had an eye to the manifestation both of his mercy and justice, Rom. 9.22-23, in order hereunto he purposed to create man upright, but mutable; and to permit his temptation and falling by sin; and to save a remnant of fallen mankind, by Jesus Christ, through sanctification of the Spirit, and belief of the truth, that his free grace might be everlastingly glorified in the vessels of mercy, which he before prepared unto glory: So also he purposed to leave the rest in their fallen state, to the wickedness of their own hearts, and justly to punish them for it, therein showing his wrath, and making his power known on the vessels of wrath, which he had endured with much longsuffering, who were fitted for destruction. Thus the end of all men is foreknown unto God, and nothing falls out casually unto him, yet is there no force put upon man, nor injustice or hard dealing from God for him to complain of.

But Mr. Collier saith, pg. 36:

> *It is dishonorable unto God, and pernicious to men; and layeth all the wickedness and plagues of the world at God's door, to affirm, as some do, that God decreed Adam's fall*

---

[12] "*By necessity of following on.*"
[13] "*By necessity of consequence.*"

before he made him; or at least so far foreknew it, as that it must be; i.e. so as to necessitate it.

An heavy charge! And we know right well who Mr. Collier intends it against: But it will be far more easy for me to manifest, that the men of his controversy have no concernment in it; than for him to vindicate his own truth and honesty; inasmuch as what they hold infers no such thing, as you may see by what I have already written of this matter, and whatsoever in his report of their opinion looketh this way, is untruly imputed to them. His best plea will be, that he slandered them by hearsay, and that himself knew not, nor understood what they affirmed of this matter; yet will not this excuse him. But to the business.

Himself confesseth, that God foreknew that Adam would fall: I ask then, could the Almighty have prevented this or not? If he could and yet did not, we conclude, that he willed or decreed, not to prevent it (though no ways approving thereof), having determined to raise glory to his own name out of it. And if the Most High decreed to permit it, and so from eternity foreknew it as future, this infers a necessity of infallibility, that in time it would so come to pass; but leaves man as a free agent to the liberty of his own will, without any coaction thereto. This notwithstanding therefore, the sin and plagues of the world, lie at the door of rebellious man. And if Mr. Collier mean by foreknowing it so as to necessitate it, such a foreknowledge or Decree of God concerning it, as in the execution thereof man should be compelled to sin, and his fall effected by God; I detest such a notion; and so do all those whom he reflects upon. And it is expected, that he either make good his charge out of their writings, or else right them by a public acknowledgement of his fault, in thus misrepresenting their doctrine.

And if Mr. Collier cannot yet conceive of a necessity of infallibility respecting the event of things, arising from the decree or foreknowledge of God, without a necessity of coaction, respecting those that are to act in the accomplishment of them, I will endeavor to help him by one plain instance, Acts 4.27-28: "**For of a truth** against thy holy child Jesus whom thou hast anointed, both Herod and Pontius Pilate, with the Gentiles and people of Israel, were gathered together for to do, whatsoever thy hand, and thy counsel determined before to be done." It is evident their design was not to fulfill the counsel of God: But thus it fell out; for whatsoever they did to the Lord Jesus, God had in his counsel determined before to be done; yea had foretold by the mouth of all his holy prophets, that so it should be, unto every circumstance of Christ's passion, viz. his crucifying, having gall and vinegar given him to drink, the parting of his raiment, piercing of his side, &c. Now either these things must so come to pass, or else the counsel of God must be disappointed, and his word falsified; will Mr. Collier then lay the murder of Christ at God's door? Were not all the agents by whose hands these things were immediately done, free from coaction, and therefore responsible for their wickedness, all this notwithstanding? And to make this yet more clear, I will transcribe a few lines from Mr. Norton in his *Orthodox Evangelist* pg. 75.[14]

> These two propositions, 1. Adam might not have sinned. 2. It could not be but that Adam would sin, are both true; and notwithstanding they may so seem, yet they are not opposite one unto the other; not being both of the same kind. Adam might not have sinned; is a categoric, or simple proposition, and is true of Adam in the sense of division, considered as in himself. It could not be but that Adam would sin, is a modal, or qualified proposition; and is true of Adam in a sense of composition, being considered as subordinate to the Decree. The Jews might have broken the bones of Christ is true; speaking in the sense of division, i.e. looking at the free will of the Jews

---

[14] John Norton, *The Orthodox Evangelist* (London: John Macock, 1654). John Norton (1606-1663) was a New England puritan held in high esteem by his contemporaries. See Cotton Mather, *Magnalia Christi Americana* (Edinburgh: Banner of Truth, 1979 reprint), I:286-302.

as in themselves: It could not be that the Jews would break the bones of Christ, is true, speaking in a sense of composition, i.e. looking at the will of the Jews as subordinate to the Decree. That answer of Elisha to Hazael, inquiring of Benhadad's recovery, containeth in it two like propositions: 1. Thou mayest certainly recover 2. Thou shalt surely die, 2 Kings 8.10; his disease was in itself curable, and as such is considered in the first proposition. The second proposition, looketh at him diseased, as subordinate to the Decree, which had pre-ordained his death, through the sifting of Hazael, by occasion of this disease.

Thus much of these things.

Mr. Collier goes on to attach another ground, and foundation of the saints rejoicing in God, who hath promised to preserve them blameless unto his Heavenly Kingdom. He propounds this question, pg. 36:

> *"May we suppose that persons who are regenerate, and born from above, may possibly fall from this state of grace?"*

Perhaps Mr. Collier hath some design in thrusting in that word ("*possibly*") into his question: I will therefore explain the term, that he may have no equivocal reserve to fly to.

A thing may be said to be possible either simply, and in its own nature; or possible on supposition of all things to be supposed with reference, to it: In the first sense it was possible that a bone of Christ might have been broken; in the latter, viz, on supposition that God had decreed and foretold the contrary, it was not so. The question in reference to the Saints' Perseverance proceeds in the last sense, whether supposing their election of God, Christ's undertaking for them and their interest in the Covenant of Grace, it is yet possible that some of them may finally depart from God, and be lost forever.

And to this I answer in the negative: But he saith:

> "*The Scriptures do not say they may not; nor that they shall certainly obtain.*"

This is false: The contrary appears from these texts, Psalm 125.1-2; Isa. 4.5; 54.8-10; Jer. 31.3; 32.39-40; Ezek. 36.26-27; John 6.39-40; 10.28-29; Rom. 8.29-30, 38-39; 1 Thess. 5.23-24; 1 Pet. 1.3-5; 1 John 2.19; with many others. He adds:

> "*We are to suppose all Gospel-believers to be regenerate, and then we may, and must suppose a possibility, for the regenerate to fall, or none can fall away.*"

By Gospel-believers I presume he intends those that are members of the visible Church of Christ; such as profess faith in him, and obedience to him, and do not at present contradict their profession by a contrary practice in the sight of men. My answer is, if we respect any particular person or persons among these, we are bound to hope so of them; because charity always inclineth to the better part: But if we respect the whole bulk of professors together, we are not to believe that they are all regenerate persons; because the Scripture telleth us, there are foolish as well as wise virgins, hypocrites, as well as sincere believers in the visible Church, though who they be we know not, till their works discover it; and when their hypocrisy is discovered, we are not to think that they once were new creatures, and are fallen from that state, but the quite contrary, 1 John 2.19. So then though many professors fall away, even such as have passed under some common work of the Spirit; this doth not at all infer, that those who are truly born again, not of corruptible seed, but incorruptible by the word of God that liveth and abideth forever, may do so in like manner. He proceeds:

> "I know nothing stated in the Gospel-law of grace, as a duty in order to obtain the end, but that persons may

obtain, and be supposed (possibly) to fall finally from, John 15.4-6."

Nothing! that's strange! Is not perseverance in faith and obedience required in order to salvation, and may persons persevere, and fall finally too? The text cited by Mr. Collier doth no ways confirm his notion, although we allow him to except perseverance from the duties intended by him; unto the fourth and fifth verses, something hath been spoken already, by which it appears that they lie directly against Mr. Collier's notion of the creature's ability of himself to do anything that is spiritually good: I suppose it is the sixth verse that he promiseth himself some relief from; the words are, "**If a man abide not in me, he is cast forth as a branch, and is withered**," &c. He doth not tell us on what account he thinks this text may serve for a proof of his doctrine, but probably he thinketh that the words suppose, that such as for a time truly abide in Christ, may afterwards cease to do so, and perish out of him; but there is no such thing intended in them: For this text (as many other do) speaketh of professors, according to what their condition appeareth to be before men, and so all that are members of the visible Church, and have a place therein, are counted branches in Christ; some of these bring forth fruit, by which the sincerity of their faith in Christ, and the truth of their being spiritually united with him is manifested; these do not fall away; but he that hath begun a good work in them doth perfect it to the end: "**The Father purgeth them that they may bring forth more fruit**:" Others of these branches do not bring forth fruit; which is an evidence that their being in Christ is only by profession, for it cannot be that one united to Christ by true faith, and the indwelling of his Spirit; should be without those vital influences from him, as will produce some good fruit; these do not abide in Christ by a lively exercise of faith, and therefore being indeed separate from him, while they appear to be one with him, they can do nothing, but in time of temptation fall away from their profession, and are cast out as branches, and are withered, and men gather them, and they are cast into the fire and are burned. And more than this cannot without offering violence to the text, be inferred from it; which doth not make against, but confirm the truth concerning the Saints' Perseverance.

That which Mr. Collier offers to strengthen his desired inference is this:

> "*The truth hereof will farther appear if we consider,*
>
> *1. That the Gospel makes no difference, but warns all to take heed of falling; which necessarily supposeth a possibility of falling with respect to us, without taking that heed.*"

That all are warned (and that very frequently) in the Scriptures, to take heed of falling, is granted; and that these warnings are sanctified and made effectual by God for the preservation of his own Elect from final apostasy, is pleaded: But Mr. Collier's inference from hence is very impertinent, and argues that he understands not their opinion that he hath undertaken to confute: He saith, that "*In respect of us there is a possibility of falling, if we do not take heed.*" Very true! It is not only possible but certain, that those which do not walk humbly, and heedfully with God, nor make any conscience of so doing, may fall away from their profession. But God according to his promise will keep his own from such a course as would ruin them: And this is all which with the Scripture we say, that God hath promised by his effectual grace to preserve all his chosen ones, all that truly believe, in a way of holiness and diligence unto eternal life. And therefore that is quite besides the business that Mr. Collier writes, pg. 35, that "*Nothing shall be able to make a breach or separation, unless we do it ourselves by sin;*" whereas God hath promised to prevent our making this breach, when he saith, "**I will put my Spirit within you, and cause you to walk in my statutes, and ye shall keep my judgments and do them,**" Ezek. 36.27. The truth is, if Mr. Collier will abide by his opinion, he must either assert, that God never loved any person, one or other; or that he is like us, changeable in his love on outward external reasons. He goes on pg. 36:

> 2. *"They have all [he intends all in the visible Kingdom of Christ] the same faith and love for kind: there is but one faith which hath the same object, and is influenced by the same Spirit, which produceth the same effect, i.e. a good conscience, even in such as fall from it."* And in the beginning of pg. 37 he adds:

> *"So that according to the law of grace, all that do believe and obey the Gospel, stand related to God therein, and nothing makes the difference, but sincerity and perseverance shall be crowned, and hypocrites and backsliders, must fall short, and meet with condemnation."*

It is well done of Mr. Collier to join sincerity and perseverance together, and so also hypocrisy and backsliding, for the latter is a certain discovery of the former. "**If ye continue in my words,**" saith Christ, "**then are ye my disciples indeed**:" And so *è contra*. But then see what confusion he hath again cast himself into: He affirmeth there is in all the same faith and love for kind, and nothing to make a difference between them, the same effect produced by the same Spirit, &c. and yet some are sincere, others hypocrites: It is strange that Mr. Collier can find out no specific difference, betwixt the lively faith of a sincere believer, and the dead faith of a painted impostor; the most holy and precious faith of God's Elect, which purifieth the heart; and the temporary feigned faith of Simon Magus, notwithstanding which he was in the gall of bitterness and the bond of iniquity.

The text which he insinuates a perversion of, is 1 Tim. 1.19, "**Holding faith and a good conscience, which some having put away, concerning faith have made shipwreck**." By faith here, as in some other places, we are to understand the doctrine of faith, the truth of the Gospel, which we are exhorted to cleave to, and hold fast, and that we may do so, we must keep a good conscience also, i.e. walk in holiness; for where that is not attended, men are not like to abide sound in the Faith, in an hour of temptation. The mystery of faith must be held in a pure conscience, "**Which some having put away**," that is, rejected, and lived in the neglect of; "**Concerning faith have made shipwreck**;" that is, have lost and relinquished, that truth which once they professed; of such he gives an instance in the following verse; but this notwithstanding, "**The foundation of the Lord standeth sure, having this seal, the Lord knoweth who are his**," &c. 2 Tim. 2.18-19. Here then is no such thing supposed as Mr. Collier intimates, that those who once had true faith, and a good conscience, did finally fall from it.

He saith farther,

> *"3. The Scripture supposeth that persons may have the same Gospel spirit in all its operations, and yet may possibly, finally fall from God, Heb. 6.4-6."*

If it were allowed Mr. Collier that true believers were spoken of in this text, he could not prove from hence, that any such shall finally fall away; the discourse being conditional, and it remaining a truth, that if a person whoever he be, or persons do depart, and fall away from God, they must unavoidably perish: Though none of the persons spoken of should do so, such expressions holding forth the inseparable connection of apostasy with damnation. And men may without any disparagement to their wisdom or reason earnestly exhort others to avoid falling away from God; though they are fully persuaded that those whom they so exhort, by the help of those exhortations, and other considerations shall abide with God to the end. But indeed it appears upon a serious view of the context that the persons here spoken of are such as have only passed under some common work of the Spirit; and that such may fall away, is not denied by any. And Mr. Collier doth without ground assert, that they have been the subjects of the same gracious work as is effected by the Spirit of God upon true believers. For:

1. Here is nothing ascribed to the persons spoken of that is in Scripture found to be the distinguishing character of true believers, which are commonly said to be "**the called according to the purpose of God, quickened, born again, justified, united to Christ, adopted,**" &c.[15]

2. The persons intended are, verse 8, compared to "the ground on which the rain falls, and beareth thorns and briars." True believers, whilst they are so, are not such as bring forth nothing but thorns and briars; faith itself being "an herb meet for him by whom they are dressed."

3. Things that accompany salvation are better things than any that were to be found in the persons mentioned, v. 9, and true believers are in this discourse of the Apostle, opposed to the persons lying under a possibility of apostasy, and are distinguished from them, upon the account of their works and labor of love showed to the name of God, v. 10, their preservation from the righteousness and faithfulness of God in his promises, v. 11, and of the immutability of the counsels of God, and his oath for the preservation of them, v. 13, 17-18. All which doth evince, that they are not the children of God by faith in Christ, of whom the Apostle speaks in the place referred to.

In pg. 37, he moves a question about the absolute and unconditional promises of the New Covenant, where he again pitifully entangles himself. It might help him a little out of the labyrinth he is lost in, if he would consider:

That the New Covenant is originally made with Christ, who

---

[15] In the margin: "See Dr. Owen of Pers. pg. 427;" John Owen, *The Doctrine of the Saints Perseverance* (London: Leon Lichfield, 1654).

became a sponsor, and surety for all that the Father gave unto him, Psalm 89.31 &c., and in him all the promises thereof are yea and amen; God the Father promised unto Christ eternal life for all his before the world was, Ti. 1.2, and engaged in time effectually to draw, and bring them unto him, to give them a new heart, &c. for whom he became surety, that they might not fail to enjoy it on Gospel terms: And this truth will of itself bear down all Mr. Collier's notions of free will, and falling from grace: It is granted that all the promises of life and glory in the Gospel, are conditional as set before us. But the fulfilling of the condition in the Elect is absolutely undertaken for in the covenant betwixt the Father and Christ. And whereas Mr. Collier saith that *"The covenant in the perfection thereof, when we are come to glory, will be absolute in all its promises; it is absolutely true to all overcomers."* He lamentably discovers his weakness thereby: For our present inquiry is after those promises that do secure the Saints safe arrival in Glory, and to talk of the absoluteness of these promises to those that are already glorified, and to represent them as uncertain to those that alone are concerned to draw comfort from them, is exceeding absurd.

In pg. 38 he frames this objection against himself:

> *"This asserts a possibility of falling from grace, and so destroys the assurance and comfort of believers:"* Unto this he answers:

> *It doth no other than the Scripture doth: It is that of which the Scripture is full: It frequently presents us with a possibility of falling: Else those many and frequent exhortations to the contrary are useless, if there were no danger, as also the examples of those that have fallen, 1 Tim. 1.19-20; 2 Tim. 1.15; Heb. 4.1. Else what means the Lord's appointing a ministry in the Church to preserve it from falling.*

That the Scripture asserts no such thing, but the contrary, we have manifested already; as also what the import of these exhortations are, and their usefulness in God's hand for the preservation of the Elect. We say moreover, if we respect our own weakness, and the temptations we are to conflict with, there is danger, but free grace will secure the Elect from perishing in the midst of their dangers, and from being overcome by all the difficulties that are in their way. And it is strange to me that he should conclude true believers may fall away, because God hath provided means, and appointed a ministry, to prevent their falling.

To the other branch of the objection, respecting the comfort and assurance of believers, he saith:

> *"It is so far from diminishing the consolation of believers, that it is the only sure way for Gospel consolation:"* &c.

I grant that none are capable of well-grounded comfort, but those that are under the promises of the Gospel, viz. sincere convert, sound believers; but how Mr. Collier will evince that his doctrine is the great spring of Gospel-consolation; even this, that

> *"Though I be now a child of God, yet the next temptation I meet with, for ought I know, may sink me to Hell; although God do at present love me, yet I have no assurance that he will continue to do so, a day to an end; for many that have been united with Christ, as I now am, are left forever; and I daily tremble under a sense of my own weakness, and have no promise of preservation to trust to:"*

I say, how this makes for their comfort I cannot understand; nor how Mr. Collier will reconcile his present opinion with what he writes in his *Body of Divinity* pg. 197: "*We ought to believe that God will maintain our faith, and keep us from falling, Phil, 1.6; 2 Tim. 1.12, else we could have no solid comfort.*"

To that which he adds in the beginning of pg. 39 concerning the usefulness of fear, I answer, the fear that ariseth from Mr. Collier's doctrine hath torment in it, and therefore a right understanding of the love of God will cast it out, and teach the soul to reject that doctrine from whence it springs: That is the true Gospel-fear, which respects God as a Father, and is tempered with an holy rejoicing in his goodness, which is a fruit of the Spirit of Adoption, that bears witness with our spirits that we are the children of God, and if children then heirs; heirs of God, and joint heirs with Christ. Moreover, there is (as Dr. Owen hath well observed, *Saints Persever.* pg. 293) a twofold fear of eternal death and destruction:

> 1. An *anxious perplexing fear* in respect of the *end itself*.

> 2. A *watchful careful fear* in respect of the means leading thereunto: The first is directly opposite to that peace, consolation, and joy in the Holy Ghost, that God is pleased to afford unto his people, and exhorts them to live up to; and therefore it cannot be his end or design to ingenerate it in them by any of his threatenings, or warnings given in his word. For the other, viz. a watchful heedful fear, for the avoiding of the way and means that would lead them, and do lead others to destruction, it is not in the least inconsistent with that assurance that God is pleased by his promises to give to his saints of their perseverance.

I shall now hasten to a close of this chapter, after I have in a word or two cleared the sense of two texts of holy Scripture, which Mr. Collier hath endeavored to darken, because they speak not according to his mind.

The first is Rom. 9.16–22. After Mr. Collier hath for a while labored against the stream of this text, he is forced, pg. 40, to acknowledge the truth, viz. that it is not our willing and running, that can bring us within the compass of special electing grace; that being past in God's will before the world was. Indeed the design of the

Apostle throughout this chapter, as well as in the verses referred to, is to show the freeness of God's grace to his own Elect, together with his just severity against the vessels of wrath; and that one is a vessel of mercy, and another of wrath, proceeds from the mere good pleasure of God to choose the one and leave the other; his choice not being grounded on foresight of their willing or running, faith, and obedience, but being purely resolved into his sovereign grace.

And this doth quite overthrow Mr. Collier's election on foresight of faith, and doth also afford a very good argument for the Saints' Perseverance, which we were last upon: But I must hasten; only it is necessary I should remove an abusive passage or two (of which his book is full) out of our way.

He saith, *"Nor may we understand that the special Elect only shall obtain, and that all others are debarred, that though they will and run, all will be in vain."*

And again pg. 41, he intimates that his opponents infer from this Scripture that:

> *God will damn whom he please from his own will and power, and save whom he will from his own will and power: Let men believe or obey, do what they will or can it is all nothing; but after all their willing, running, repenting, believing, obeying, watching and warring, they must leave all to the eternal will and power, &c.*

This is as notorious a slander, as he could well have cast upon them; for all they say, amounts to no more than this, that the election have obtained, and the rest are blinded: And this we are bold to affirm still, having so good warranty for it as we have, though he go on to reproach us therefore. But that we say, willing and running, believing and obeying, &c. is in vain to the non-Elect and that after all watching and warring, the state of men must be determined by the eternal will and power, is a very gross, and I fear a studied untruth, there being no foot-steps of any such assertion to be found in the doctrine or writings of the men of his controversy. It being constantly asserted by them, that there is an inseparable connection between faith and salvation, and that it is an everlasting truth, that he which believeth shall be saved, and he which believeth not shall be damned: and it is as true; that none do will or run after a right manner but the Elect, who are drawn with lovingkindness, because loved with an everlasting love. It is in vain for Mr. Collier to pretend to be a follower of peace and holiness, whilst he makes no conscience of belying and abusing those, that have no otherwise offended him, than by a sober asserting of those truths, that the corruption of his heart riseth against.

And whereas he saith, pg. 40, "*It condemns all willing and running, without having respect to the mercy of God in the Gospel, leaving out Christ, and grace,*" &c. This is a truth in itself, though not the direct sense of this text, that all such running will be in vain. But I desire to know how he will reconcile this with his other doctrine, of the salvation of very many that know not Christ, nor the grace of God as revealed in the Gospel.

The other text is 1 John 2.19, "**They went out from us, but they were not of us; for if they had been of us, they would no doubt have continued with us; but they went out that they might be made manifest, that they were not all of us.**"

This text is so express against the falling away of true believers, that Mr. Collier despairs of dealing with it, on any fair terms;[16] and therefore instead of an exposition, adventures upon a down-right contradiction to it. The Apostle saith, that by persons going out from the true Church it is manifest they never were living members of it; and that God suffers such to fall away, that so their hypocrisy might be discovered. Mr. Collier saith, "*John might know it some other way; and that this proves not that all that may go out from the Church were not of them.*" The text saith again, "**If they had been of us, they would no doubt have continued with us.**" Mr. Collier saith nay, "*Some may go out, who if they had continued might, yea must have*

---

[16] In the margin: "*Additional Word*, pg. 44"

obtained," i.e. were once sincere: John saith, if it had been so, "**no doubt they would have continued.**" Now let the reader choose whether authority he will embrace.

Audacia—
Creditur a multis fiducia.[17]

And if Mr. Collier shall still object (as probably he will) that "*It is not to be desired that men should persist in their hypocrisy, neither is there any danger of falling away from it,*" &c. I answer in the words of Dr. Owen, *Saints' Pers.* pg. 295:

> Though they may not be exhorted to continue in their hypocrisy, which corrupts and vitiates their profession, yet they may in their profession which in itself is good: And though there is no danger of leaving their hypocrisy, yet there is of their waxing worse and worse, by falling from the beginnings of grace which they have received, the profession which they have made, and the regular conversation which they have entered upon.

So that notwithstanding anything said to the contrary, the Scriptures insisted on to prove the saints' final apostasy, may principally belong to some kind of professors, who notwithstanding all their gifts and common graces which they have received, yet in a large sense may be termed hypocrites, as they are opposed to them who have received the Spirit with true and saving grace.

I shall close this with my earnest request to Mr. Collier that before he adventure on a farther opposition to this great truth, he would seriously peruse the book referred to, and diligently consider, the strength of what is there pleaded by the reverend author for the doctrine of the Saints' Perseverance; which if he would do, I am persuaded the profit, or at least, conviction of the weakness of his

---

[17] "*Audacity (presumption)—it is believed by many to be honest confidence.*" In other words, people take Collier's presumption as deep trust.

present arguments against it, which he might receive thereby; would (even in his own judgment) abundantly compensate his pains: However, it will farther inform him, what he hath to remove out of his way, before he can establish the doctrine now asserted by him, and so may guide and influence him to speak more pertinently, and modestly, than hitherto he hath done in a matter of so great importance.

CHAPTER VI

Of Justification

That article of our faith which concerns the justification of a sinner in the sight of God, must needs be acknowledged to be of great importance, and we ought to be more careful of nothing, than that our minds be not corrupted from the simplicity of the Gospel, and we moved from our steadfastness thereabout, and therefore although Mr. Collier in the book before me hath said but little directly to that point, yet observing divers things therein very opposite to, and inconsistent with the truth in this matter, I could not pass them without some remark.

And in the first place I shall briefly propose what the Scripture teacheth us, and then examine Mr. Collier's notions that are contrary to the truth revealed therein.

The term "Justification" is constantly in the Scriptures speaking of this matter taken in a Law-sense, as it imports the acquitting of a person by the sentence of a judge. The Justification of a sinner by God, is:

"The gracious sentence of God by which for Christ's sake apprehended by faith, he looseth the sinner from his obligation to eternal wrath and punishment; and accounts him righteous to the obtaining of Life and Glory."[1]

1. It is the sentence of God as a judge acquitting, Rom. 8.32.

2. It is a gracious sentence without any respect to our worthiness, or works of righteousness that we have done or can do, Rom. 3.24; Eph. 2.8-10.

3. The meritorious cause of our Justification is the obedience of Christ both passive and active;[2] and our actual Justification is the effect or consequent of the imputation thereof unto us. Justification in the formal reason thereof, doth speak two things.

    1. A discharge from condemnation; or, the remission of sins; which was purchased by the death and blood-shedding of Christ; Gal. 3.13; Eph. 1.7. The benefit of which purchase redounds to us, because of God's reckoning upon our account, or imputing to us what our surety suffered in our stead, Isa. 53.6, 11.

    2. The adjudging of us to be heirs of, and so inrighting us in, Life and Glory, for the sake of Christ's active obedience imputed to us in like manner, Rom. 3.22; 4.4-5; 5.19; Gal. 2.15; 3.11-12.

---

[1] This quotation is probably Coxe's translation/paraphrase from the Latin of Ames' *Medulla* cap 27. The Latin text reads "Iustificatio est sententia Dei gratiosa, qua propter Christum fide apprehensum absolvit fidelem à peccato & morte, & justum reputat ad vitam." Amesius, *Medulla* S.S. Theolgiae, 138 (chapter 27.6).

[2] In the margin: "Voet. Select. Disput. pars 5. pg. 281," a reference to Voetius's, *Selectarum Disputationum*.

3. [3] True and lively faith whereby we receive Christ and his benefits freely given of God to us, and rest on him and his righteousness, is the instrument of our Justification, John 1.12; Rom. 5.17. So that faith alone justifieth (though justifying faith is never alone, but worketh by love) and that righteousness for the sake of which we are justified before God, was wrought out and fulfilled only by Christ; who was made sin for us, although he knew no sin, that we might be made the righteousness of God in him. And therefore in the business of Justification, faith is opposed to all good works, as exclusive of them from any influence into the obtaining of our pardon and acceptance with God, Rom. 3.20-22, 28; 4.4-5; Gal. 2.16; 3.11-12.

The first mention of this article, that I meet with in Mr. Collier's book is ch. 1, pg. 12, where after some boasting of his clear stating the matter in his *Body of Divinity*, he thus writes:

> *If any persons dare to maintain, that any are justified before God without faith and holiness; as the terms thereof, though not the deserving cause; I must leave them to their own understanding without all Scripture grounds; for my own part I fully, on good grounds, believe the contrary.*

Notwithstanding Mr. Collier's swelling words of vanity, and contempt of the understanding of others; I must tell him, even these words are not so clear and scriptural, but that they give just occasion to suspect his own understanding to be dark, and his judgment to be unsound. For although true and justifying faith is pregnant with good works, and whosoever is justified is sanctified also; and that faith

---

[3] The original reads "4."

considered as a grace inherent in us, belongs to our sanctification: Yet doth not the Scripture anywhere allow good works the same influence into our Justification as it doth unto faith; which is a clear evidence that it is not the act of believing, nor any other holy duty for which we are justified: But that in this business, faith is to be considered as relative to Christ, and that it is the object of faith apprehended thereby on the account of which it is said to justify. And this Mr. Collier cannot but own, if he understands what is asserted by himself in his *Body of Divinity* concerning the imputation of Christ's righteousness unto us in order to our Justification before God; for if we are justified freely by grace, and are presented without spot before God in an imputed righteousness, then can our good works have no interest in the reason of our acceptance with him. And indeed if this were not so, we could not be justified at all, forasmuch as the "**Lord is of purer eyes than to behold iniquity**;" and our sanctification is imperfect, so that if all our righteousnesses, so far forth as ours be examined in strictness of justice, they will be found but filthy rags, a covering too narrow, and a bed too short. Yea if those that plead most for the interest of good works in our Justification, would seriously consider what themselves dare abide by before the tremendous tribunal of the great Judge; they must all fly to *Bellarmines tutissimum est*,[4] and put an end to this controversy, by acknowledging that they dare not venture into God's sight, nor pass out of the world to his

---

[4] This is a common post-reformation shorthand reference to Cardinal Bellarmine's remarkable acknowledgement that we ought not trust in our own works but in the grace of God alone. It was well-known and frequently referenced with this simple phrase. John Owen provides a fuller quotation of the original and a translation: "*Propter incertitudinem propriae justitiae, et periculum inanis gloriae, tutissimum est fiduciam totam in sola misericordia Dei et benignitate reponere*," Bellar. de Justificat., lib. 5 cap. 7, prop. 3; — "By reason of the uncertainty of our own righteousness, and the danger of vain glory, it is the safest course to repose our whole trust in the mercy and kindness or grace of God alone." John Owen, *The Doctrine of Justification by Faith* in *The Works of John Owen* (Edinburgh: The Banner of Truth, 1981 reprint), V:32. The quotation in context may be found at *Disputationum Roberti Bellarmini ... De Controversiis Christianae Fidei Adversus Hujus Temporis Haereticos* (Venetiis: Joannem Malachinum, 1721), 504.

Judgment-seat in their own righteousness.

But indeed there is another principle laid down once and again by Mr. Collier in those chapters of his book already examined, which (if true) renders all discourses of deliverance from wrath to come by Christ needless, and without ground; It is this, that:

> *"The penalty of the breach of the first covenant, was only temporal death, and eternal damnation is inflicted on men only for sinning against the Gospel, the Law of Faith."*

Now if this were true, besides that in some respects it renders the condition of those that never heard of Christ more eligible than those who live under the sound of the Gospel:

> 1. If there be no law threatening eternal death, but the Law of Faith, then there is no such thing as forgiveness and remission of sin in the world;[5] for the Gospel denounceth damnation only against final impenitency and unbelief; and as these are not pardoned nor pardonable, so on the other hand, if there be no law threatening eternal death besides the Gospel, then is there no other sin we need forgiveness of.

> 2. If this be true, then Christ never died to free any from wrath to come (which yet is plentifully asserted in the Scriptures, wherein we read also that his death was for the Redemption of the transgressions that were under the first covenant, Heb. 9.15). For it is nonsense to say that he hath freed us from the curse of the Gospel; yea it is a

---

[5] In the margin: "Ferg. Differ. of Moral Virtue and Grace, pg. 107." This is Robert Ferguson, *A Sober Enquiry into the Nature, Measure, and Principle of Moral Virtue* (London: D. Newman, 1673). Ferguson (1637-1714) was for a time an pastoral associate of John Owen. See the entries in the *Dictionary of National Biography* and the *Oxford Dictionary of National Biography*.

> repugnancy, unless you will introduce another Gospel to relieve against the terms of this, nor will that serve the turn, unless you likewise find another mediator to out-merit this.

Thus Mr. Ferguson, in answer to one of Mr. Collier's mind.

So then if Mr. Collier will abide by this notion, and the just consequences thereof, his sense of our justification must either be contradictory to himself, or else very corrupt and unsound.

Another passage that hath a bad aspect this way, you meet with *Additional Word*, pg. 50, where he gives this reason why his supposed deliverance of the damned will not extend to any degree of Glory, but only a deliverance from pain and misery, *"For they are under no promise of reward of good works, because they had none."*

That God will graciously reward the good works of believers, is granted, so that besides that joy and glory that all Saints have an immediate right to by virtue of their interest in Christ, every one shall receive a superadded crown, according as his work shall be; which layeth a foundation for our believing the enjoyment of different degrees of glory among the blessed in another world. But to suppose, as Mr. Collier here doth, that the admission of persons into the Kingdom of God is for the sake of their own good works, is contrary to the whole current of Scripture, and cannot consist with a sound judgment concerning our justification; but necessarily leads to a Popish or Socinian notion thereof. I cannot see what good works the Thief upon the Cross had to procure his admission into the Kingdom of God; yet he being freely justified by grace, went immediately from the cross to paradise.

To conclude this; no less offensive is that passage we meet with, pg. 59:

> "The Protestants to be rid of Popish meritorious works, run themselves too much in both principle and practice, beyond almost all works of charity."

This hath a long time been the clamor of the Jesuits against the faithful ministers of the Gospel, and for Mr. Collier's joining with them in this calumny and slander (of which neither he nor they can ever make proof, at least so far as concerns their doctrine) there is no reason; but their refusing to advance the good works of men into the room of Christ, and to assign unto them, what we are alone beholding to his righteousness for. On other accounts none plead the necessity of good works, nor press men to holiness with greater earnestness, and force of Scripture reason than they do, as cannot but be known to all that are conversant in their writings. And therefore public satisfaction for this reproach cast (not on particular persons, but) on the whole Protestant interest, is justly expected from Mr. Collier.

But however, forasmuch as it appears that Mr. Collier is little acquainted with the wholesome doctrine of orthodox Protestants, I will give him a taste of what they teach concerning the necessity of good works. In *Synopsi purioris Theologiae*, written by Polyander Rivet, Wallæus and Thysius (no obscure men amongst the Protestants).[6] After they have in their 33rd chapter laid down, and abundantly confirmed that truth concerning our justification, which I have before touched; in the 34th chapter, they professedly treat of our holiness or good works, which are the fruits of a lively and justifying faith; concerning which they say §. 24:

---

[6] Johannes Polyander, André Rivet, Antonius Walaeus and Antoine Thysius, *Synopsis Purioris Theologiae* (Leiden: Elzevier, 1642). These men were members of the faculty at the University of Leiden. Johannes Polyander (1568-1646) was a Dutch theologian who was a student of Franciscus Junius and Theodore Beza and edited the Canons of Dort. See John McClintock and James Strong, eds., *Cyclopædia of Biblical, Theological, and Ecclesiastical Literature* (New York: Harper Brothers, 1894), XII:779-80; André Rivet (1572-1651) was a Huguenot scholar and minister who fled France to the Netherlands. See Nehemiah Coxe, *A Believers Triumph over Death, exemplified in a Relation of the Last Hours of Dr. Andrew Rivet* (London: Benjamin Alsop, 1682); Antonius Walaeus (1573-1639) was a pastor, Bible translator and participant at the Synod of Dort. See McClintock and Strong, *Cyclopædia*, X:853; Antoine Thysius (1565-1640), a student of Theodore Beza, and participant at the Synod of Dort was appointed to the Leiden faculty in 1619. See Rochus Lillencron *et. al.* eds., *Allgemeine Deutsche Biographie* (Leipzig: Duncker & Humblot, 1912), XXXVIII:239.

Necessitas bonis operibus multifariam tribuitur. Necessaria enim dicuntur, 1. Necessitate præcepti, divini. 2. Necessitate medii, ad Dei gloriam & salutem nostram ordinati. 3. Necessitate cultus & obsequii, Deo ex obligatione nostrâ naturali, debiti. 4. Necessitate bonæ & tranquillæ conscientiæ, de sua electione & vocatione ad salutem sibi probe consciæ. 5. Necessitate officii charitatis proximo præstandi.	*The sense is this, Good works are necessary on divers accounts: They are said to be necessary, 1. Because commanded of God. 2. They are necessary as a medium ordered (or in order) to the glory of God, and our own salvation. 3. They are necessary, in that they are the worship and obedience that we are by the law of nature obliged to perform to God. 4. They are necessary for the keeping a good and peaceful conscience, comfortably witnessing to our election of God, and calling unto salvation. 5. They are necessary on the account of that office of love, that we ought to perform unto our neighbor."*

I might heap up testimonies of this kind; and will at any time, if called to it, evince from the confessions of faith of all the reformed Churches, and from the writings of all the worthy reformers that treat of this subject, as also from theirs who of late have asserted our justification by free grace through the imputation of Christ's obedience both active and passive to us, without the works of the Law, that they all plead for a necessity of good works on the account, and for the ends, beforementioned. So then their doctrine deserves not this calumny; and if any have not practiced according to their principles and profession, let them bear their own burden and shame; however, I suppose it is easy to manifest, that nowhere under Heaven is impiety of every kind more abundant, than amongst the Popish merit-mongers. And I must say again, that as the writings of Protestants need no advocate in this matter, they sufficiently speaking for themselves, so in this charge of Mr. Collier's against them, thus causelessly printed to the world, and accommodate (though perhaps not designedly) to help forward the ruin of the Protestant interest, and introduce Popery, he hath raised a monument of his own petulancy and ignorance, that will remain to his shame as long as his book is in the hands of men, to be read by them.

CHAPTER VII

Of the Day of Judgment, and the Everlasting Punishment of the Wicked

I am now come to the chapters in Mr. Collier's book, wherein he treats of the Day of Judgment, and the punishment of those that then come into condemnation; concerning which his notions are so corrupt, and accommodate to give countenance to, and encourage men in, a wicked course of life in this world, by suggesting, yea affirming that this notwithstanding, there is hope for them in another world; that scarce anything could have been written more opposite, and destructive to the Christian religion, and the main design of the Gospel.

I shall (according to my former method) briefly propose what the Scripture teacheth concerning this fundamental article of the Eternal Judgment; and then remove out of the way what he hath opposed thereto. The Scripture teacheth,

1. That there shall most certainly be a solemn and set day, or

time of judgment, in which God will judge the world in righteousness by Jesus Christ, Acts 17.31; Rom. 14.10; 2 Cor. 5.10.

2. All persons of high and low degree, good and bad, must appear before his Judgment-seat, and receive their sentence from him, Matt. 25.32, &c.; 1 Pet. 4.5; Rev. 20.12.

3. All the actions, words and thoughts of men in this world (though now never so secret), must then be brought to light, and accounted for, Prov. 24.12; Eccl. 12 *ult*; Matt. 12.36-37; Rom. 2.16; 1 Cor. 4.5.

4. Sentence shall be passed upon all according as their works shall be found to have been, and every man shall receive what he hath done in the body, according to what he hath done whether it be good or bad. As is abundantly proved by the texts cited before. But yet:

The works of the saints, and the works of the wicked, fall under a different consideration in this day, for:

> 1. The works of the Godly are not considered as meritorious of Heaven, which is assigned to them for an everlasting inheritance by the sentence of the great judge: Luke 17.10, but only as the fruits and evidence of a true and lively faith in Christ, unto which salvation is promised for the sake of his merit.
>
> 2. The works of the reprobate world are directly considered, as deserving in their own nature the punishment to be inflicted on them, and they are accordingly proceeded against, Rom. 6, *ult*.

Thus all nations are divided into two companies: The sheep are set on the right hand of Christ, and the goats on his left. The first are sentenced to eternal life, and the other to everlasting wrath; and accordingly these shall go away into everlasting punishment, but the righteous into life eternal, Matt. 25.

Mr. Collier begins to discourse of this matter in the sixth chapter of his book: Some things dropped therein, have been already answered, and therefore I shall only stay to mind the reader, that although the Scripture speaks of different degrees of the punishment of sinners, according to the different measures of iniquity which they have filled up; yet it everywhere assures us that the punishment of all sinners that are found without an interest in Christ, at the Day of Judgment, shall be everlasting; as shall more fully be evinced in my reply to his next chapter. And whereas he here speaks something of the condemnation of those that sinned against the Law, and never had the Gospel tendered to them, either before or since Christ came in the flesh; it is very doubtful to me, whether he honestly speak out his mind in this matter, seeing he hath so stiffly maintained before, that "*The penalty of the breach of the first covenant was only temporal death; and that damnation is the punishment of Gospel-disobedience only; which they cannot be guilty of, which never heard the Gospel.*" If this be true, I am sure such must not now come into condemnation. But whatever Mr. Collier will, or will not allow, we are sure of the truth of the Scripture; which teacheth other doctrine, as hath been already proved against him; which if he will subscribe to, he must of necessity recede from this corrupt notion.

We are now come to his seventh chapter, pg. 47, where he first proposeth this inquiry:

> "*Whether there may be any probability from Scripture light, of any deliverance from, or mitigation of the punishment of any, after the sentence is past, and the judgment executed.*"

Which he thus answers:

> *"Touching this I do apprehend that there are probable grounds both from Scripture and reason, that there may be a deliverance of some from the penal part, or pains inflicted, though not from the sense of loss; the judgment in that respect will be eternal."*

Although it be exceeding sinful for a man, though with the greatest pretense of modesty, to suggest that which is opposite to a fundamental doctrine of the Christian religion, and on that account Mr. Collier's pretext of proposing his notion on *"probable grounds,"* will not excuse him; yet besides this, you shall find him to be most positive, and peremptory in his assertion of what he here pretends to lay down only as a *"probable supposition;"* and that in the very next sections; which is a full evidence that this pretended modesty of his, serves only for a bait to the hook, which is by him let down to take simple souls; which renders his design so much the worse, and the more blameworthy.

The sufferings of the damned, have by the School-men (not improperly) been distinguished, *in pœnam sensus, & pœnam damni, into the punishment of sense, and punishment of loss*,[1] the one is signified in those texts that speak of their being **"shut out from the Kingdom of God,"** and the like; the other of those that speak of their being **"cast into a lake that burneth with fire and brimstone,"** their being **"tormented day and night,"** &c. But that there is any part of their punishment which is not penal; and that this punishment of loss, is to be distinguished from that which is so; is such a contradiction, as I think is peculiar to Mr. Collier, who hath here furnished us with this distinction. Thus we may see, **"The beginning of the words of his mouth is foolishness; and end of his talk is** (like to prove) **mischievous madness,"** Eccl. 10.13.

And whereas Mr. Collier supposeth the duration of their punishment of loss, who are damned, shall be eternal, but not that of

---

[1] Coxe's translation.

sense; he is utterly without any probable ground in Scripture or right reason for his opinion. For although their suffering be sometimes expressed negatively, and sometimes positively, yet there is no intimation of the separating of the positive part from the negative, so that some persons shall eternally be punished with the loss of good, but not with the feeling of evil. But both are in Scripture inseparably linked together, both with respect to the subjects of them and their duration. "**Who shall be punished with everlasting destruction from the presence of the Lord, and the glory of his power,**" 2 Thess. 1.9, which certainly speaks the punishment both of sense and loss, and the duration of both to be alike. And that the positive part of their punishment, or (as Mr. Collier terms it) their "*pain inflicted*" shall be eternal, the Scripture is express, which saith more than once, that they shall "**go into Hell, into the fire that never shall be quenched, where their worm dieth not, and the fire is not quenched**," Mark 9.43-44, &c. For the chaff Christ will burn up with "**unquenchable fire**," Matt. 3.12, and "**The smoke of their torment ascendeth up for ever and ever,**" Rev. 14.11.

Let us now see what countenance Mr. Collier gives to his notion; His first plea is:

> *The Scripture lets us know that some shall be saved, that through their own miscarriages, shall lose the reward of their own work, 1 Cor. 3.14-15, 'They shall be saved yet so as by fire;' and what that fire is, and how far it shall extend, at and after the Judgment, I must leave to him that knoweth all things, to determine, &c.*

This text is by the Papists abusively applied to their Purgatory, and it must be acknowledged their reasoning from it, hath as much probability as Mr. Collier's, though both they and he do miserably wrest it. He confesseth that he neither knows "*what this fire is, nor how far it shall extend.*" He may well excuse us therefore, if we refuse to take this, for any proof of his notion. That the fire here mentioned, is not to be taken properly, but metaphorically, is evident from the Apostle's discourse, which is wholly in terms used, figuratively, viz. wood, hay, and stubble, to signify such works as will not abide trial; gold, silver and precious stones, to denote those that will. So by fire, we are to understand, such a probation of men's works, as will be like fire unto the gold, stubble, &c. burning up the one, and manifesting the excellency of the other: And seeing Mr. Collier in his following lines (though without giving any sufficient reason therefore) doth reject the interpretation of those, that refer this to any time or trial before the Day of Judgment; I will not contend with him thereabout; but granting its respect to that time, consider what must then be the true meaning of the text; which can be extended no farther, than to signify to us:

1. That in the great day every man's work shall be strictly examined, and proved of what sort it is.

2. That those works which have not been wrought in God, all labors bestowed in a wrong way of doctrine or practice, will then be burnt up, and prove unprofitable to those that have wrought them.

3. That it is possible that some who are themselves built, and do build on the true foundation, may yet so far err in their work, at least some part of it, as that it may not be approved in this day, but must be lost, even as wood, hay, and stubble is consumed by the fire; and they miss of that reward which shall be given to those, whose labor hath been better employed, in the promoting of sound doctrine and godliness, to the glory of God, and the profit of their own and others' souls. And:

4. That this notwithstanding, those that have an interest in Christ, and have been in the main sincere with God, shall "**themselves be saved; yet so as by fire**," they cannot escape this trial of their

work, and loss of that superadded gracious reward, which they should have received, if they had built upon the foundation gold, silver, and precious stones.

Now let the whole context be diligently read and weighed by his reader and mine, and I doubt not but he will see that Scripture proves not at all the salvation of any that die in their sins, after the final sentence is passed upon them.

And here it may not be unseasonable to remind Mr. Collier, of those rules of interpreting Scripture, that he would seem to have some regard to pg. 39, viz.

1. Not to understand any dark Scripture contrary to the plain revealed will of God in his word.

2. Not to understand any Scripture so as to contradict others, especially so as to contradict the volume of the book of God.

This himself confesseth must needs be corrupt and dangerous, and yet everyone may see that his business throughout this chapter is to oppose some few sayings of Scripture, that have some difficulty attending their interpretation, with parabolical and figurative expressions, corrupted by his false glosses, unto a multitude of plain texts, and the whole scope of the Scripture bearing plentiful witness to the certainty of the everlasting punishment of the ungodly.

But I shall proceed. He saith again:

> *The Lord of all lets us to know that none shall be eternally damned, but those who sin against the Holy Spirit, Matt. 12.31. Three of the Evangelists state this for confirmation, Mark 3.28; Luke 12.10. And if all sin shall be forgiven, then there must be a deliverance from the Judgment.*

Now is Mr. Collier's mask of pretended modesty put off, and laid aside; and instead thereof a daring assertion of his heresy is introduced, and that by him boldly entitled to the "*Lord of all,*" which oweth its original to the Father of lies, viz. "*That none shall be eternally damned, but those who sin against the Holy Spirit;*" and that he may at once give full proof of his confidence, he adds, that this is stated by three of the Evangelists; whereas in truth there is no such thing, so much as intimated in any one of them; but in divers texts of Scripture, the Lord of all lets us know, that many shall be eternally damned for other sins, that may not be chargeable with the sin against the Holy Ghost; unto those already pleaded, you may add Rev. 20.15; 21.8.

As for the texts abused by him; the scope and design of them plainly, is to let the malicious revilers of Christ and his miracles know, that although the grace of God to sinners is so abundant, that all sin and blasphemy of those that truly repent and believe in Christ may be, and to some hath been and shall be, forgiven on the terms aforesaid; yet those that willingly and maliciously reject and blaspheme Christ, so doing despite to the Spirit of grace, whereby they have been so far enlightened as to know, that what the Gospel reveals concerning Christ and salvation by him is truth, are utterly excluded from hopes of pardon, or possibility of salvation; it being impossible to renew them to repentance, and there remaining no more sacrifice for sin. Compare the texts cited with Heb. 6.4-6; 10.26-29. The words in Matt. 12 are:

> Verse 31, "**Wherefore I say unto you, all manner of sin and blasphemy shall be forgiven unto men; but the blasphemy against the Holy Ghost, shall not be forgiven unto men.**"

> Verse 32, "**And whosoever speaketh a word against the Son of Man it shall be forgiven him; but whosoever speaketh against the Holy Ghost, it shall not be forgiven him neither in this world, neither in the world to come.**"

The same thing is intended in either of these verses, though the expression thereof be doubled for the greater certainty, and remarkableness thereof.

"**Wherefore I say unto you**," this refers to what is before recorded, v. 24 &c.

"... **all manner of sin and blasphemy**," i.e. sin and blasphemy of every kind; not every individual sin and blasphemy: The adultery of repenting David was forgiven, but not the adultery of those mentioned, Rev. 21.8. The blasphemy of Paul, and the words that he spoke against the Son of Man, but not of Caiaphas, Herod, &c. "**shall be forgiven unto men:**" And so v. 32, "**it shall be forgiven him**," i.e. it is remissible; by the grace of God through Faith in Christ, it may be forgiven, and to some it hath and shall be forgiven. Verbs that signify action are sometimes understood only of a faculty or power of action; so Psalm 22.18, "**I may tell all my bones**:" In the Hebrew it is, "**I will tell all my bones.**" The sense is well expressed in our translation. And Prov. 20.9, "**Who can say, I have made my heart clean**," &c. In the Hebrew it is "**who saith.**" Many will say and pretend this; but the meaning is, who of right can say so. And that the words should here be taken in this sense, the analogy of faith doth require.

"... **but the blasphemy against the Holy Ghost**;" or "**whosoever speaketh against the Holy Ghost**," i.e. whosoever blasphemeth wittingly and maliciously, against the inward enlightening, and conviction of the Spirit;

"... **shall not be forgiven unto men**;" and v. 32, "it shall

not be forgiven him neither in this world, neither in that which is to come." Thus you have the certainty of their damnation first absolutely expressed, v. 31, and then emphatically repeated in such terms as may serve farther to cut them off from all hopes, and exclude all possibility of their forgiveness, v. 32. And in them no more is intended than was before expressed; and is in like absolute terms expressed by the other Evangelists: No intimation (which Mr. Collier vainly imagines, pg. 48) that any which are not forgiven in this world, may obtain pardon in that which is to come.

It is certain that it was a familiar phrase with the Jews to call the age of the messiah the world to come, and some with great probability to accept this sense both here, and in Heb. 2.5; 6.5, which if admitted, gives this interpretation of the place; that although by Christ believers are justified from all things, from which they could not be justified by the Law of Moses; yet in the Gospel is there no remedy provided for them that sin against the Holy Spirit, but that transgression remains unpardonable, both under the Law and under the Gospel. Nay moreover, if we allow Mr. Collier that forgiveness in the world to come is in these words intimated; yet neither will this relieve him; for the Apostle speaks of the blotting out of the sins of believers at the coming of Christ; and it is certain that then the sentence by which they are now absolved will be published before men and angels, and they possessed of the utmost advantages accruing to them by their pardon; so then declaratively they are forgiven in another world; but none have or can have an interest in this forgiveness, but those that have repented and been converted in this world, Acts 3.19-20.

Indeed if we allow Mr. Collier this notion, that sinners shall be forgiven after they are damned, we must grant him more than what he yet openly pleads for, viz. that they shall not only be delivered from the positive part of their punishment, but the negative also: For he whose sins are forgiven is a blessed man, and certainly interested in the favor of God. But it is in vain to expect that notions so opposite to truth as Mr. Collier's are, should be brought to any consistency.

In pg. 48, Mr. Collier forms and answers this objection:

> *"This Scripture only supposeth that on repentance, all such sins may be forgiven; not that they shall be forgiven without repentance."*

In his answer hereunto he grants:

> *"That we may not suppose the forgiveness of sin first or last to be without repentance."*

It seems then that the forgiveness in another world, which Mr. Collier dreams of, is attainable on the same terms on which it is offered in this, and no other; which is not only repentance, but also faith in the Lord Jesus. So that according to his principles, after the Judgment is passed, sinners are still upon the same terms with God as they are now in the day of his patience; than which supposition, nothing can be more false, and repugnant to the Scripture: "**Now is the accepted time; now is the day of salvation**." And if poor sinners do not "**seek the Lord while they may be found, and call upon him while he is near**," Isa. 55.6, it will be too late in another world; for then although "**they call upon him he will not answer**;" they may "**seek him early but cannot find him**." See Prov. 1.24-31. When death hath once turned us off the stage of this world, our day is past, and the night is come "**wherein no man can work**," John 9.4; Eccl. 9.10. There will be no more repentance unto life then or possibility of changing our state, but every man must eternally reap the fruit of what he hath sown in this life. As there is no promise for the damned to hope in, or Gospel to be preached to them, so neither shall they have any more a call to repentance, or tender of mercy forever. He adds:

> *"And that there may be forgiveness and acceptance after death, seems*

farther to appear: Else what means 1 Pet. 3.19-20 with chapter 4.6?" In 3.19-20, it is said, *"by which also he went and preached to the spirits in prison, which sometimes were disobedient,"* &c. Thus far Mr. Collier repeats the words, but omits the rest, which are, **"when once the long-suffering of God waited in the days of Noah, while the Ark was preparing; wherein few, that is, eight souls were saved by water."** Mr. Collier is here quite started from the thing in question, viz. whether the damned may be released from their torment, after the Day of Judgment; and instead of proving that, talks of forgiveness after death before that day come, which is short of the task undertaken by him, though as contrary to the whole tenor of Scripture. The meaning of the words wrested by him (so far as concerns the business in hand) is, that Christ by his spirit in Noah (for thereby were the prophets of old acted, 1 Pet 1.11) who was a **"preacher of righteousness,"** 2 Pet. 2.5, went and preached to the old world, whose spirits, for their disobedience, were now in the prison reserved to the judgment of the great day. But against this, two things are objected by Mr. Collier:

> *"1. It is said he went, i.e. Christ, not his spirit only by Noah."*

The text saith indeed **"He went,"** but fully explains also the *manner how he went*, viz. by his spirit; as God is frequently said to speak to those unto whom he sent his prophets, so is Christ here said to preach to the old world, by his spirit in Noah.

> *"2. He does not say he went by Noah to the people of the old world, but he went and preached to the spirits (not persons) in prison: Noah's preaching was to persons living, this to the spirits in prison."*

The former part of this objection is answered already, and the scope of the text doth inforce the sense I have given of it; and whereas Mr. Collier saith this preaching was *"to the spirits, not persons in prison*," &c. it is a mere quibble; for the Apostle speaks of them according to their present condition when he wrote this: He doth not say they were spirits in prison when preached to; but that the spirits of *those persons* were *now* in prison, unto whom Noah preached while they lived in the world.

And therefore that suggestion of Mr. Collier's is utterly groundless, that "*It is greatly doubtful whether this be it which is here intended.*"

But however, if it were only "doubtful to him;" it leaves him inexcusable, in his bold adventure to pervert it as he doth. Certainly if the time of the preparation of the Ark was "the time of God's long-suffering," towards them unto whom Noah preached by the spirit of Christ, there was no pardon to be expected for them, or offered to them after that time. Neither can any reason be given why this should be restrained to those that were disobedient in the days of Noah, if ever the "pardon of sinners after death" had come into the Apostle's mind; for we may not suppose that these were privileged above all others that died in their sins.

And although Mr. Collier saith a little after, that "*This doth not justify the descending of Christ's soul into Hell, as some hold*;" yet it must necessarily infer, that Christ in person descended into Hell, which is as absurd, if not more.

> *3. And especially, compare this with ch. 4.6, which seems to be the same with this: For, for this cause also was the Gospel preached to them that are dead, that they might be judged according to men in the flesh, but live according to God in the Spirit. Where the Apostle states these things: 1. That the Gospel was preached to them that are dead: 2. The time when it was preached to them, that was, after they were dead.*

Although it be granted that in some respects this text is hard to be understood; yet it is most easy to evince, that it gives no countenance to Mr. Collier's notion; neither doth it seem, that the same persons with those intended, ch. 3.19, are here spoken of, but rather such as the preaching of the Gospel had a far better, even a saving effect upon; and Mr. Collier's saying that the time when the Gospel was preached to them, is by the Apostle determined to have been "*after they were dead*," is utterly false. He saith indeed, "**The Gospel** εὐαγγέλιον[2] **was preached**," or "**hath been preached**," i.e. in the time past, "**to them that are dead**," i.e. are now dead; they were dead when Peter wrote this, but alive when the Gospel was preached to them. I need say no more to evert Mr. Collier's design, but it may not be amiss to make a little farther inquiry into the meaning of this text. It is evident from the context, that the design of the Apostle is to press those to whom he wrote unto sanctification, and conformity to Christ, which doth consist in their dying unto sin, and living unto God, v. 1-3. And in verse 4 he meets with an objection, by which they might be retarded in their course of obedience, viz. that if they did not conform to the world, they must expect to become their grazing stock, and to suffer hard things from them; which he fortifies them against, by remembering them of the Day of Judgment, in which ungodly sinners must be accountable for all those wrongs which the godly have received from them, v. 5, and this judgment is illustrated by the distribution of the object, "**the quick and the dead**." And from the occasion of this distribution the Apostle urgeth another argument against that discouragement which might arise from persecution; because it had been the lot of others unto whom the Gospel had been preached afore time, and they had yielded obedience to it, "**to be judged according to men in the flesh**;" i.e. to be censured and condemned according as the malice of men did dictate to them, in this world; which they did patiently bear, and through much tribulations did enter into the Kingdom of God, the great design of the Gospel being accomplished upon them, in their "**living according to God**," in a conformity to him and his will, in the Spirit; i.e. in the exercise of grace and holiness, under the conduct of the Holy Ghost,

---

[2] "*Gospel*" or "*Good news.*"

who is the fountain of that spiritual life which is begun in the saints here, and perfected in Glory. The end and effect of the preaching of the Gospel to believers that were dead, was the same, as unto those that then lived, viz. that though they did meet with suffering, they should persist in their duty of living to God. A like manner of speaking we have: Rom. 6.17, "**Thanks be to God that ye were the servants of sin, but yet have obeyed**," &c. i.e. though you were; for it is that expressed in the close of the verse, which was the ground and occasion of the Apostle's thanksgiving, viz. their obedience: So the great end of Gospel preaching is, that men may live to God, though the cross will fall in their way. I know some do interpret the former sentence of the latter part of the verse otherwise, as holding forth mortification, and the last vivification, so taking the whole of our sanctification to be expressed by them together, which I shall not oppose, it being the sense of those far more learned and judicious than myself, but at present my own judgment is most determined in the sense given; which divers of great worth, have also embraced before me. But to return; Mr. Collier still pleads for his corrupt sense of the first words of the text.

> *"That it is apparent from these expressions; 1. It was preached to them that are dead."*

Wherein the evidence of this expression lies, Mr. Collier doth not declare; we read in Ruth 1.8 of Naomi her daughters in law, "**dealing kindly with the dead**," i.e. with their husbands who were dead when Naomi spoke this, but certainly their dealing kindly with them, was while living; and in the verse before this, is mention made of the Judgment of the quick and the dead: Shall we hence conclude, that any shall remain dead in the Day of Judgment?

> *"2. That they might be judged according to (or as) men in the flesh, viz. that they were judged, in this matter, as if they had been alive in the flesh, which imports they were not."*

It is plain that ἵνα κριθῶσι "*that they might be judged*,"[3] must intend, either conviction, or censure and condemnation, not account or esteem of persons as if they were, what they are not, as Mr. Collier doth imagine; neither is it ὡς ἄνθρωποι, "*as men*" (according to his gloss) but κατὰ ἀνθρώπους,[4] "*according to men;*" the sense of which hath been already given; so that Mr. Collier's inference being built on this false gloss, hath no weight in it, but it still remains certain, that they were alive when the Gospel was preached to them. What follows in this section needs no farther reply, but is fully answered in what I have already written.

The next ground urged by him, pg. 49, is as followeth:

> *The Scripture presents us with the deliverance of Sodom and Gomorrah in some time, from the greatness of their judgment; and of Samaria, Ezek. 16.46 and 49, he promiseth a restoration to them both, out of their forlorn estate, v. 55, 61. This is spoken of literal Sodom, and cannot be mystically applied.*

Here are two things supposed by Mr. Collier without any proof offered:

1. That in this Scripture *literal* Sodom is "*spoken of,*" &c. But if we take the words as they are read in our translation, I conceive he can give no reason why they should be applied to literal Sodom, more than for the understanding of the promise literally, that they shall return to their former estate, which none shall do in this world, after death; much less after the Day of Judgment.

2. He supposeth that the promise of restoration made to the

---

[3] Coxe's translation. A marginal note: "An old version put forth in K. Edwards time reads it 'that they should be condemned of men in the flesh.'"
[4] Both phrases are immediately translated in the text.

Jews, &c. must be applied to those particular persons that perished under the stroke of God's wrath; than which nothing is more absurd; for the bulk of the people then in being, were threatened with utter destruction, and there was but a remnant that should escape, which God would still own, and make good these promises to. Indeed some passages in the close of this chapter may most properly be referred to Gospel times; and were never intended, as promises to all the seed of Israel after the flesh (as the Apostle argues at large in the Romans), but to the Church, the spiritual seed, although the Israelites shall have a large share in them, when the desired day of their calling, and returning to God is come; but their claim of right in New Covenant blessings, must now be on the account of their faith in Christ, not their natural descent from Abraham.

Let us now look into the text: And first we find, that when the Prophet enters upon this comparison of Jerusalem with Samaria and Sodom, v. 44, he saith, "**Everyone that useth Proverbs, shall use this Proverb against thee**," &c. which doth plainly lead us to a metaphorical sense of divers terms used in this proverbial, or parabolical discourse. Yea he saith, v. 45, to the Jews, "**Your mother was an Hittite, and your father an Amorite**:" Which certainly is not to be taken in a literal sense, but is rather intended to note their corrupt manners than their natural descent. And so although in the name Sodom there is an allusion to literal Sodom, and the punishment thereof, yet may we rather understand the Moabites and Ammonites to be intended, who were like to Sodom and Gomorrah in their sinfulness, and in their punishment. See Zeph. 2.9. And there seems to be some farther occasion of this allusion, not only in the situation of these countries near to the land where Sodom stood, but more in that they sprang from Lot, who was once an inhabitant among the Sodomites, whose evil manners his posterity did now conform to. And indeed we find this in Scripture to be a common brand of great sinners: See Job 36.14; Isa. 1.10; Rev. 7.8. Now many of these two nations did return to their country, as divers of the ten tribes did also, when Judah returned; but especially are these promises made good in Gospel times, in the gathering of Jews and Gentiles into one Church, under one head Christ Jesus. And these things duly weighed, lead to such an interpretation of this prophecy, as is according to the analogy of faith, and fully agreeing with other texts, both which are crossed and contradicted, together with the whole scope of the text under consideration by the sense that Mr. Collier would force upon it. For:

1. It is evident that the promises here made must have their accomplishment in this world, which is the only time and place for godly repentance, and entering into covenant with God by faith in Christ.

2. The Scripture and reason doth cut off all hope of the returning (so much as) of any remnant of literal Sodom, see Isa. 1.9, and saith expressly, that the Sodomites do suffer the vengeance of eternal fire, Jude 7, which passage Mr. Collier mentions a little after, I suppose to prevent others objecting it against him, for certainly he cannot be so ignorant as to think that it strengthens his sense. No doubt those that suffer the vengeance of eternal fire, are cut off from all hope of deliverance.

3. The grace promised in v. 62, 63, is not a deliverance from torment only, but a full and free pardon, and taking of the persons pardoned into covenant with God, which includes their enjoyment of him as their portion, which, by Mr. Collier's own grant, is no ways applicable to the damned in Hell.

And it is evident that the tolerableness; allowed unto Sodom in the Day of Judgment, [Matt. 10.15] [The original mistakenly reads Matt. 18.15.] (which he pleads) is only comparative; they shall be tormented less than those that have rejected the Gospel. And the reasoning of our savior in that, and like texts, is to this purpose, that "The condemnation of the Sodomites will be great, is easily granted by you, because they were great sinners; and you are promising to yourselves a far better portion than theirs is like to be in the Day of Judgment; but do not deceive yourselves, for your sin in rejecting the Gospel, is greater than any they were guilty of, and your punishment (if you go on to neglect so great salvation) will be heavier than theirs. It shall be more tolerable for them, in the Day of Judgment than for you." And there is no force of reason or terror to the persons threatened, suitable to what is intended, if according to Mr. Collier's notion, pg. 53, *The day of general judgment should be the day of Sodom's ease.* That they should not be then condemned, but released from their punishment, and escape the judgment that the rest of the wicked world fall under. If this assertion of his be not bold and anti-Scriptural, I know not what deserves to be so accounted.

Mr. Collier proceeds to argue:

> *Why may we not suppose that God may in time be pacified towards sinners, after they have born their sin and judgment, as formerly be hath declared himself to be, or will be in time to come, Ezek. 16.58. Seeing God hath been or will be pacified in judgment, why should we suppose him to be unreconcilable, and never to be pacified in this last and great Judgment?*

Is there indeed no difference betwixt the state of men in time, and in eternity? Why then can Mr. Collier see no reason against sinners' expectation of the same mercy hereafter, as now some do partake of in the pardon of their sins, and salvation by Christ? Men are now under a mixed dispensation of justice and mercy, and the time of life in this world is the only time of God's patience, 2 Pet. 3.9, and while this time doth last, he doth as well design the reclaiming of sinners by temporal judgments, as the vindicating of his own holiness, and therefore when this is accomplished, he may be here, and ofttimes is pacified towards sinners. But in the world to come this mixed dispensation ceaseth, and the vessels of mercy shall enjoy the fruit of mercy perfectly and only; and the vessels of wrath the extremity of justice, all that is then designed towards them, being "**the making known of wrath, and glorifying justice**" upon them, Rom. 9.22-23. They must drink the wine of God's "**wrath without mixture**," Rev. 14.10. And therefore no hope for them after this last and great Judgment.

He proceeds; *"The Scripture saith expressly, that God is the savior of all men, but especially of those that believe, and it is not present outward salvation that the Apostle is there speaking of,"* &c.

The text referred to is 1 Tim. 4.10, where the Apostle is giving an account of his diligence, and constancy in the work of the ministry, notwithstanding the persecutions that did or might attend him on that account, as also the encouragement he had there to; because "**he trusted in the living God, who is the savior of all men, especially of those that believe;**" which can intend no other than the conserving providence of God, which is over all, and especially his own people: So the 70 render Psalm 36.6: ἀνθρώπους καὶ κτήνη σώσεις κύριε; "**Thou wilt save** (or preserve) **men and beasts O Lord.**"[5] It is evident the Apostle encourageth himself in that salvation that is presently enjoyed in this world, who is the savior, &c. and if Mr. Collier's corrupt sense of this text be admitted, I cannot see how he will exclude those that have sinned against the Holy Ghost, otherwise than by an arbitrary exception of his own; for every man is partaker of the salvation here intended.

In the 7 §. pg. 50, Mr. Collier repeats again who it is for whom he intends this deliverance from Hell-torments; But with his vain words we are not concerned, being well-assured, there is no such thing, and that distinction insisted on, §. 8, we have already proved

---

[5] "The 70" is a reference to the Septuagint, the Greek translation of the Old Testament. The Greek phrase is translated in the reference to Psalm 36.6.

to be vain and groundless. Those that are under the Eternal Judgment, must suffer eternal torment as well as loss. And indeed (according to this man's principles) they may as well expect deliverance from the one as from the other; for those that have forgiveness of sin, have also righteousness imputed to them; and are on that account received to glory, not for their own good works; the want of which he makes the only bar unto the admonition of these persons into the Kingdom of Heaven.

Yea he asserts farther, §. 9, that "*This favor and mercy shall be extended to them on the account, and for the sake of Christ,*" and again, pg. 54:

> *"Why we should make that an argument against all grace after the judgment (the infinite sacrifice remaining the same to have its influence herein) which hath been our alone hope and help before the judgment—I do not yet understand."*

It is pleaded that sin is against an infinite majesty, and therefore deserveth everlasting punishment; and this Mr. Collier acknowledgeth to be true; but yet saith, that God is infinite in grace as well as in justice, and therefore this property of God can be no bar to the relief of the damned; and then pleads, that "*The infinite sacrifice of Christ remains the same to have its influence for the obtaining of grace after the judgment of before.*"

Now if this be so, either Heaven was never purchased by Christ for those that believe in this world, or the damned have through the influence of his sacrifice, as free access thither, upon their repentance as we. Nay, if Mr. Collier will suspend it on men's good works, seeing they may repent when damned, why may they not do other good works also to such a measure as to earn Heaven as well as we?

But behold here another instance of his daring confidence in asserting his anti-Scriptural and pernicious notions! Where is the Scripture that saith Christ died for the redemption of the damned in Hell? Or that his sacrifice was ever designed for the obtaining of grace for such as die in their sins? It is most certain, that when the great Day of Judgment is passed, the Lord Christ hath finished all his work as mediator, and will then present his Church complete before God, and so give up the Kingdom to the Father, that God may be all in all, 1 Cor. 15.24, &c. There will therefore remain no more sacrifice for sins pleadable for the remission of any that are not already saved, but their redemption ceaseth forever. And although sinners in the day of God's patience, are invited and encouraged to come to him on the account of his infinite mercy in Christ, yet is it nowhere proposed as a ground for hope, or spring of comfort to the damned, who are the objects not of mercy, but divine vengeance.

In the last place he pleads that *"This is rational and most God like, who hath let us know that he will suit his judgments to men's various facts for measure."*

That is most rational and becoming God, which he hath revealed in his word, and it is the highest presumption to dictate unto him another way, for the manifestation of his glory upon the vessels of wrath, than himself hath fixed on. **"Who hath been his counsellor?"** Himself also hath revealed, that as a righteous Judge he will suit his judgments to the various facts of men, and that some **"shall be beaten with many stripes, others with few,"** Luke 12.47-48. But this difference of punishment doth not consist in a differing duration, but present degrees of torment; their fire that have sinned ignorantly shall not be so hot, as theirs that have sinned willfully, neither will their worm gnaw them so grievously; yet of both it is true, that their **"worm never dies, and their fire is not quenched."** He adds:

> *"From the same reason and rule of righteousness, hath he given us hints of limitation in respect of time, as if he would not be forever punishing: Luke 12.58-59. And this word till, or until in Scripture rarely imports eternity, but limits to time, Matt. 18.34-35; 5.25-26."*

That we have any hint in the Scripture of limitation, in respect of the time of the punishment of the wicked, is false. And that reason and righteousness do render such a limitation necessary, is audacious boldness to assert: Is God unrighteous who taketh vengeance? Shall vile dust be so bold, as to fix the demerit, and limit the punishment of an offence against the infinite Jehovah! But Luke 12.59 is brought in to give countenance to this abomination: The words are, "**I say unto thee, thou shalt not depart thence until** καὶ τὸ ἔσχατον λεπτὸν ἀποδῷς,[6] **thou shalt have paid even the last mite.**" Apply this now to the case of sinners in the prison of Hell, as Mr. Collier doth; And:

1. It utterly overthrows his notion of their release by forgiveness, on condition of repentance, through the influence of Christ's sacrifice; no such thing can be admitted in this case, no favor is to be expected, but even the last mite must be paid, or no release can be obtained.

2. It most emphatically sets forth their irrecoverable and everlasting damnation; for if they may not expect any mercy, but must themselves pay the utmost mite they are indebted to divine justice, we know they must be paying it forever, it being impossible for a finite creature to satisfy the demands of an infinite God, justly provoked to anger by our rebellion against him; so in the other texts mentioned "**until**" being referred to, and determined by that which never can be done, doth utterly cut off all hopes from those that are once fallen into the hands of the living God; and so by consequence doth necessarily infer an absolute denial of the thing spoken of. See 1 Sam. 15.35. And this is directly the scope of the parable, to take men off from their presumptions of relief in another world, and to press them now to make their calling and Election sure. And if it may be thought that men may satisfy divine justice,

---

[6] A translation immediately follows the phrase.

and pay the last mite, I know not but the devils may possibly do so too; and may as well as men, on this account, justly claim a release from their torments, sooner or later.

Thus far I have considered and removed what Mr. Collier offers for the countenancing of his new doctrine, and by reason of my having already exceeded the room I intended to have comprised this reply in, I shall be forced only to touch upon divers things that are behind in his book. The next work which (all in vain) he addresseth himself to; is an endeavor to obviate those objections that may be made against his notion of the Judgment, some of which have already been inforced, and his cavils answered; others of them are laid so slightly (I suppose), that he might make some show of answering something, as scarce anybody besides himself, would have so expressed their mind; and with these I shall little concern myself, only the second must be insisted on when we come to it.

The first objection Mr. Collier takes notice of, is that which he supposeth may arise from those texts that affirm, "**but few shall be saved**," Matt. 7.14; Luke 13.24.

It is certain that more maybe collected from such sayings, than ever he is able to remove out of his way; for if there be but two sorts of men, viz. the little flock of Christ, his Church which shall be saved; and the goats, the world of ungodly which shall be damned, then may we in no wise admit (what he hath before asserted) that "*multitudes shall be saved, that are not espoused to Christ;*" or that "*None shall be eternally damned but those that sin against the Holy Spirit.*" Let us hear what he saith to these things.

First he grants, that "*Few enter in at the straight gate,*" &c. but then adds:

> "*Though sluggish Christians and formalists enter not in at the straight gate, yet this proves not that they shall find no mercy at all: If so, woe will be the case of most of professors at that day.*"

There is no middle way, if persons enter not in at the straight gate that leadeth to eternal life, they must go in at the wide gate that leadeth to destruction; and if their names are not found in the book of Life, they must be cast into the lake that burneth with fire and brimstone, where they are tormented forever and ever. Yea but if there be not some provision made against this rigor; formalists, yea the most of professors will be in an ill case; and the foolish virgins are not like to obtain so great a privilege in this day as Mr. Collier hath before allowed to them, and therefore he concludes his opinion must be admitted. This in plain terms is no less than to accommodate his doctrine to give countenance to the wickedness of men: Formalists are hypocrites in the midst of their profession, and they shall be so far from finding mercy in that day, that their case will prove worst of all: see Matt. 24, the last verse. And how many soever they be that are in that day found without the wedding garment of faith and true holiness, they must (however they may now trust to lying words, and make much of the pillows that Mr. Collier soweth under their Arm-holes) "be cast into outer darkness, where there is weeping and gnashing of teeth," Matt. 22.12 &c. And it will then be manifest to the eternal woe of formal professors, that "**many are called but few are chosen.**"

The second objection is thus laid down by him, pg. 51.

> *"The Scripture sentenceth the wicked with eternal damnation, assuring us that it shall be everlasting, Matt. 25.41, 46."*

This in my judgment is utterly unanswerable, unless Mr. Collier's testimony prevail against that of the Scripture. That the everlasting punishment of the wicked is plentifully asserted therein, is manifest, and a cogent proof hereof we have in the text instanced, Matt. 25.41, and 46. In v. 41 we read, that the sentence which Christ will pass upon the wicked in the great day, will be, "**Depart from me ye cursed** εἰς τὸ πῦρ τὸ αἰώνιον[7] **into everlasting fire** (or, into that everlasting fire; for the doubling of the article adds emphasis to it) **prepared for the Devil and his angels:**" Observe here, they are sentenced not only to eternal loss, but eternal torment also, to everlasting fire, even that everlasting fire that is prepared for the Devil and his angels: As the children of God being the children of the Resurrection, cannot die any more, but are ἰσάγγελοι,[8] equal to the angels, Luke 20.26, or in a condition of immortality and blessedness without change, even as the blessed angels are; so the damned are in the same condition with the devils, as to the unchangeableness thereof, and duration of their suffering. An account of the issue of this judgment we have v. 46, "**And these shall go away** εἰς κόλασιν αἰώνιον, **into everlasting punishment; but the righteous,** εἰς ζωὴν αἰώνιον,[9] **into everlasting life.**" And here we find nothing of the sentence abated, but are assured of its execution in the full extent thereof. The persons condemned being driven away from all good, and cast under divine wrath, and punishment in Hell fire, which is everlasting; of the same duration with the life and happiness of the righteous. For the same word (both here and in other places) is used to express the duration of both, and that in such wise as can no more admit of limitation with respect to the one than with respect to the other; everlasting life, and everlasting punishment, being constantly and directly opposed to each other. We will now consider Mr. Collier's answer. He saith:

> It is evident that Matt. 25 intends professing Christian nations; for others cannot be accused and sentenced for not showing kindness to Christ in his members,—and so may be such as under the sound of the Gospel, sinned against the Holy Spirit, or such as may obtain a time of mitigation.

That only professing Christian nations are intended in this text,

---

[7] The translation immediately follows.
[8] "*Like or equal to angels.*"
[9] The translation of both phrases immediately follows.

is utterly false, and against the express terms thereof: "**Before him shall be gathered all nations**," v. 32. Mr. Collier saith, "*Others cannot be accused for not showing kindness to Christ in his members*:" We grant it; but must they not therefore appear before his Judgment-seat? And may they not be accused and sentenced for other sins? Mr. Collier may as well infer from this text, that professing nations shall be accused and sentenced only for sins of omission, seeing no other are here mentioned, as that other nations shall not be concerned in this sentence. It was evident that Christ's design was not to enumerate all the sins, that men shall be condemned for, but only to give instance in some, which they to whom he then spoke, were immediately concerned in. But if this were granted, Mr. Collier he is still in as bad case as before, for certainly thousands that die in their sins, even where the Gospel is preached, are yet never guilty of the sin against the Holy Ghost: To solve this he tells us, "*such may obtain a time of mitigation*;" although the text say, that all which were set on the left hand of Christ, shall go away into everlasting punishment. Thus by contradicting the text, he hath boldly adventured to cut the knot which he could not untie. He proceeds:

> *Eternal, everlasting, and forever, being understood according to the common use and import of the word in Scripture, seems rather to confirm this understanding than otherwise; for we must understand it according to the time or times intended, and not always forever without end, but very often the contrary, and that both in the Old and New Testament.*

Mr. Collier could have said nothing more against himself, than what he hath here written; for if these words are to be interpreted according to the subject matter (which he calls, "*the time or times intended*"), then certainly when they are referred to that state which succeeds time, when duration shall be no more measured by days and months and years, but time shall be swallowed up in eternity, they can denote no less, than "**forever without end.**" Moreover that these terms are most commonly used in this sense, both in the Scripture and among it men, cannot be denied: And when a thing is said in Scripture to be everlasting, we cannot on any account suppose it shall have an end, unless it be in one of these two cases:

1. When the duration of that thing is expressly limited to some time, in other texts, or:

2. When the subject to which anything said to be eternal, is attributed, is not capable of an absolutely eternal duration, at least in that condition, wherein alone, this may be attributed to it.

And thus it is, in all those texts where these terms are used in a limited sense in the Scripture; as anyone may clearly see, that shall read the places cited by Mr. Collier or others like to them. Now this will in no wise warrant his restriction of them in the present case. For:

1. They are (in reference to the punishment of the wicked) nowhere limited throughout the book of God.

2. Mr. Collier himself confesseth, that wicked men shall remain in being forever: So then here is an unlimited threatening of everlasting punishment to be inflicted on a capable subject; and for any man to say that less is intended, is a blasphemous contradiction to the Scriptures. Indeed the eternity of the torment of wicked men, is expressed by all those phrases in the word of God, that are most significant of a duration without end; so that nothing can be spoken more, than is therein contained for the clearing this matter.

Mr. Collier proceeds to instance in some texts where "**forever**," and "**everlasting**," are used in a limited sense in the Old Testament; which limitation hath already been considered, and the reason of it fixed; But he seems to lay special weight on Jer. 7.7 and 25.5, "*where,*" he saith, "*forever and ever must be thus understood.*"

There is the like reason for the limitation here, as in the other texts, that speak of "**serving forever**," and "**an everlasting Priesthood**" of Aaron, &c. and till Mr. Collier can produce evidence of the same reason, and necessity to admit a limitation with respect to the punishment of sinners, he saith not one title to the purpose: In both these places the Israelites are told, that on condition of their obedience to God, they should enjoy their Land, למן עולם ועד עולם which we render "**forever and ever**,"[10] the 70 exactly ἐξ αἰῶνος καὶ ἕως αἰῶνος: i.e. "**from age to age**;" or "**from generation to generation**," as long as they and their offspring remained in the world: But there is another phrase used in the Hebrew to signify an absolutely eternal duration, viz. לעולם ועד which by the 70 is rendered very commonly, εἰς τήν αἰῶνα τοῦ αἰῶνος;[11] and to express the same thing are these words used oft in the New Testament; and are rendered "**forever and ever:**" Yea three times is the duration of the torment of the wicked expressed by them therein; and that the phrase might be more emphatical, they are put in the plural number, εἰς τάς αἰῶνας τῶν αἰώνων[12] the significance of which we cannot reach in our language: This you find Rev. 14.11; 19.3; 20.10. And I am well assured, neither Mr. Collier nor any of his Socinian masters, can produce one place in the New Testament, where these words in such a connection, may be taken in a limited sense.

---

[10] Literally "*from long age unto long age.*" The Hebrew prepositions in this compound phrase turn the reader's attention back to the distant past and forward to the distant future in order to express a long, indefinite period of time, like an eternity. (cf. 1 Chr 16:36; 29:10; Ps 41:14; 103:17; 106:48; Jer 7:7; 25:5 of the Masoretic Text).

[11] Literally "*to long age and there unto.*" The Hebrew prepositions in this abbreviated phrase do not turn the reader's attention back to the distant past, but only forward to the distant future and another distant future beyond that. Thus, this phrase, sometimes occurring without the first preposition, expresses an unending, eternal future. (cf. Exod 15:18; Ps 9:6; 10:16; 21:5; 45:7, 18; 48:15; 52:10; 104:5; 119:44; 145:1, 2, 21; Dan 12:3; Mic 4:5 of the Masoretic Text).

[12] Literally "*unto the ages of the ages.*"

To his discourse concerning the words αἰών & αἰώνιος,[13] I shall briefly make this answer:

1. That αἰών is πολύσημον,[14] a word of many significations, is granted; and therefore must be interpreted according to the scope of the place where it is used; although it cannot be denied but oft-times eternity is signified thereby; as in John 6.51 and 58 (with divers other places), where it is used to express the eternal duration of the life and blessedness of believers; and in Mark 3.29, the everlasting misery of those that have sinned against the Holy Spirit, is expressed thereby. And for Mr. Collier to instance in those texts where it is not directly expressive of time; but the duration of things created in time, as Matt. 28.20, or doth signify the course of men in this world, as Eph. 2.2, to prove that it may be taken in a limited sense, when it strictly imports the duration of something, in another world, when "**time shall be no more,**" is mere trifling. But he saith, "*Not only* αἰών, *but also* αἰώνιος, *which are the common words for everlasting, and forever, yet must frequently be understood with limitation,* &c. αἰώνιος, *sometimes intends the time before the world was, sometime the time of a man's life, Phil. v. 15.*"[15]

I suppose Mr. Collier will grant, that the use of this word, Ti. 1.2 and Rom. 16.25, where it is to be considered *a parte ante*, is that wherein we are not concerned in our present disquisition: It is therefore incumbent on him to prove, that when it is used to signify duration (*à parte post*)[16] yet to come, it is frequently to be taken in a limited sense in the New Testament; and that it must be so taken

---

[13] "*Age*" and "*age-long.*"
[14] "*Has multiple senses.*"
[15] N.B., Philemon, verse 15.
[16] "*A parte ante* and *A parte post*. Scholastic expressions for those aspects of the eternal life of God whereby it is thought as without limits in the past (ante) and in the future (post)." See https://psychclassics.yorku.ca/Baldwin/Dictionary/defs/A4defs.htm.

when predicate of the torments of the damned. This last (which alone would relieve him) he despairs of, and therefore silently passeth over; and gives but one instance of the first; in Phlm. v. 15, "**That thou shouldst receive him** αἰώνιον, **forever;**" which we grant to be an hyperbolical expression, denoting as long time as they lived together; and the reason of this limitation is clear in the text; He could not longer enjoy him as a servant. A like saying to this we meet with in an heathen poet:

Serviet æternùm, qui parvo nesciet uti. Horat.[17]

Not one place more can be produced, where such a limitation of the sense of this word may be admitted; and yet it is used about 70 times in the New Testament. And therefore Mr. Collier doth woefully prevaricate when he saith, "*it must frequently be thus understood.*" Indeed the common use of it is such, as (Mr. Collier himself being judge) will admit of no limitation: Sometimes it is put to signify the everlasting being, glory and blessedness of God himself; and about 50 times or more, in the New Testament, is the eternal duration of the saints' life and happiness in another world, expressed thereby; and frequently the everlasting torments of the wicked is so also; as hath been before urged, and every one may see how preposterous a course it would be, because the term is once used figuratively in a limited sense, which the subject there treated of, and scope of the place doth inforce; therefore to limit it in all other places where it doth occur, although there be not only no reason for it, but also in the things spoken of, an utter repugnancy to such a limitation. And if Mr. Collier know these things already, he is far from upright dealing in this business: If he know them not, he is guilty of great temerity in publishing such things as these to the world at all adventures.

Much more might be added, but I must hasten.

In the last branch of his answer to this objection, pg. 52, he hath

---

[17] "*He will be a slave forever, who does not know how to live on little*" (lit. "*to use little*"). This is a quotation from Horace Epistles I.X.

recourse again to his former distinction, and allows the judgment of the wicked to be eternal in respect of their loss: But the vanity of this, hath been already detected, and my answer thereto need not be here repeated.

The next thing he attempts, is to clear his doctrine from a charge laid against it most justly, viz. that it tends to the encouragement of sinners in their wicked ways. And truly this is so evident in itself, that it needs no farther inforcement; yea in his answer he lays a farther ground for such a charge; His words are these,

> *"If a fit of sickness and terrible pain, be so hard to be born here for a season, in which men wish for death, and cannot obtain it; what will be the dreadful state of sinners that must lie in the fiery lake, some perhaps a 100, some a 1,000, and some perhaps 10,000 years," &c.*

Thus he will interpret everlasting punishment, to be lying in the fiery lake perhaps an hundred years; yea according to his principles, perhaps it may not be an hundred days, no nor an hundred hours neither; for if they repent (which he supposeth they may and shall do) the sacrifice of Christ remains the same to procure their pardon then as now; and no doubt he will allow them the same power and free-will to repent there as here, so that as soon as they find the place displeasing to them, they may repent, and repenting may obtain mercy, and deliverance out of it. And if this were true, there is nothing can be devised more effectual to encourage a wicked life; as on the contrary, the doctrine of Eternal Judgment doth make sinners tremble: And by it they are restrained from much wickedness which otherwise they would rush into: See also 2 Cor. 5.10-11.

Mr. Collier is aware also that some will tax him for complying with the Popish doctrine concerning Purgatory, and therefore, pg. 53, he endeavors to show the difference betwixt his Purgatory and theirs.

I cannot now stay to run the parallel betwixt them; but must tell him in short:

1. That although his doctrine of a "Purgatory after judgment" be not so pernicious to men's purses, as the Papists have rendered theirs, yet it is full as much, if not more ruining to their souls that shall receive it, and they that follow either of these blind guides; and content themselves to go out of this world without faith and true holiness, on hopes of a time to repent and better their state hereafter, will certainly fall into the ditch of eternal woe and misery, and their heavy curse will (all too late for their own relief) come upon those that seduced them with this vain hope, that will prove as the giving up of the ghost.

2. On two accounts, his doctrine in this point is more gross than the Papists; for:

    1. They make believers, *fideles*[18] (supposed to die in venial sin) the subjects of their Purgatory; but Mr. Collier will indulge the Sodomites, yea all that have not sinned against the Holy Ghost, to pass through his Purgatory unto forgiveness and ease.

    2. They place their Purgatory before the last Judgment and final sentence; so that they do not so directly oppose that fundamental article concerning the Eternal Judgment, as he doth; nor suppose any possibility of sinners obtaining a change of their condition after the sentence is passed by the great Judge, which yet Mr. Collier hath the boldness to plead for.

There are other unsavory notions couched in his answer to this objection, viz. that ordinarily sinners cannot come under any

---

[18] "*The faithful.*"

judgment, or suffer any punishment before the great day, &c. But I must pass over them at present; only, mind how contrary this is to what we are taught in Luke 16.23; 1 Pet 3.19, &c.

The last objection that I shall be concerned to take any notice of, is to this purpose:

If the damnation of the wicked be limited unto time, why may not the salvation of the godly be so likewise?

Now although Mr. Collier pretend that there is not the like reason for the one as for the other, this will not secure us of the possession of this truth. For if his arguing were right, we had no word in Scripture that assures us of eternal glory. There being no term used therein to signify the everlasting duration of the saints' happiness, but what is used to denote the duration of sinners' torment; which Mr. Collier will not allow to be without end: And, as he hath today pretended reasons for limiting the words in this respect; so may another idle brain tomorrow, devise as good reason for limiting the duration of the believers happiness; and then where are we in this point, seeing the eternity which the Scripture speaks of after Judgment, may (in this man's sense) have an end in one hundred years?

In Mr. Collier's eighth chapter he pretends to give some reasons of his understanding the Scriptures abused by him as he doth: But they being urged on those false grounds, which have been already detected and refuted, I will not abuse my reader's patience to attend my second, or farther raking into such an heap: But shall oppose thereto some reasons, why his notion of the judgment and punishment of sinners must be rejected, briefly summed up from the former discourse. I shall begin with his own words, pages 1-2.

1. *"For any to affirm that which the Scripture doth not, must needs be unsound and unsafe."*

But the Scripture nowhere affirms, nor allows, that persons may obtain forgiveness after they are damned, and by repentance get out of Hell-torments, &c. Ergo, Mr. Collier's assertion hereof (by his own confession) must be esteemed unsound and unsafe.

> 2. That assertion, which is contrary to the express terms, and evident scope of the holy Scriptures, in a fundamental article; is pernicious and heretical.

But this doctrine of Mr. Collier's is such; ergo, it is pernicious and heretical, and is so, to be rejected by all that love truth, and tender the safeguard of their own souls.

The first proposition I suppose will not be denied, and the second, is abundantly proved in the foregoing lines; unto which you may add Heb. 6.2, where you read, that this truth concerning the Eternal Judgment lies in the foundation of our religion. And it is evident that it is called the Eternal Judgment; because the sentence then pronounced is unalterable, and bindeth forever: The condition of men is finally determined thereby, and they left under an impossibility of obtaining any change thereof (either in whole or part) to eternity.

> 3. That doctrine whereof the just and necessary consequences, are absurd and contradictory to Scripture, is so itself.

But such is the doctrine of Mr. Collier concerning forgiveness after death, &c. Ergo:

The *major* I think cannot be opposed with any color: It is a sure maxim, *Ex veris nil nisi verum*.[19] The just and necessary consequence of a true notion, is truth, and nothing else.

The *minor* is in part proved before; and shall be now farther inforced by an instance or two.

> 1. If Mr. Collier's notion be admitted; the day wherein we must

---

[19] "*From true [things] nothing [comes] except [that which is] true.*"

all appear before the Judgment-seat of Christ, is not the last day (though called so John 12.48; James 5.3), nor can that be accounted the final judgment: For he measures the damned sinners enduring of torments, by days and years after that; and allows no eternity of them, but that which perhaps may expire in an hundred years; and then they experience a change in their release from them; which release cannot certainly be obtained without a second sentence of the Judge past concerning the persons discharged; yea his notion admits of a *vicissitude of changes in infinitum*, after that judgment, which in Scripture language is the last, hath passed upon men. For if they are capable of repenting so as to obtain forgiveness, then by the same reason we may conclude a possibility of their sinning again to condemnation, and so repenting again, &c. which doth infer that men are in no fixed state in another world; and also that infinite sentences may be passed upon them (according as they change their manners) after the Judgment of the great day.

2. His opinion supposeth another Gospel, wherein provision is made for the relief of the damned, and doth contradict all those texts, that speak of the present Gospel ministration, as the only day of God's gracious visiting sinners, and making order of mercy and forgiveness to them.

3. It lays a foundation not only of praying for the dead, but the damned also. If favor and mercy may be extended to them for the sake of Christ, as he hath asserted, we have the same reason, and so the same warranty to pray for them; as is by the Apostle urged for our praying for all men while living in this world, 1 Tim. 2.

But why do I detain my reader with a particular account of the absurdities that flow from this man's opinion, which yet he would have us think to be most rational? *Dato uno absurdo, mille sequentur.*[20] I will break off here, and leave others to collect those that remain, in their own thoughts of these things, and speedily put a period to these lines.

To his ninth chapter where he tells us what use he supposeth may be made of his doctrine; I shall make no farther reply; but having already proved his doctrine to be corrupt and unsound; I conclude that it must needs be not only useless, but also pernicious to the souls of men.

I shall close all with one word, 1. to professors, 2. to open sinners:

First, unto those that profess subjection to Christ, and are found walking in his ways, I make it my earnest request, and that not in my own but Christ's name, that they labor after steadfastness in the faith and profession of God's truth, especially in such a day as this, wherein many speak perverse things to draw away disciples after them: And in order hereunto, that they cry mightily to God to make their hearts found in his statutes, and content not themselves with a bare assent to truth, but receive it in the love thereof; that they may in their own breasts have that testimony to the power and efficacy thereof, which alone will secure their profession, in an hour of temptation; and that they be careful as well to hold forth the doctrine of Christ, by a life conformable thereto, as by confessing it with their tongues.

Secondly, to those that live in their sins, I would speak in the words of the prophet, **"Can your heart endure? Or can your hands be strong in the day wherein God will deal with you?"** Oh remember how fearful a thing it is to fall into the hands of the living (sin revenging) God! Who can dwell with devouring fire, with everlasting burnings? Be persuaded therefore by them that know the terrors of the Lord, to seek him while he may be found, and to call upon him while he is near: Oh what would the Christless man give in exchange for his soul, when he sees there is no remedy, but he must have his part with the Devil and his angels, in the fire that is not

---

[20] *"One absurdity being allowed, a thousand follow."*

quenched! But repentance, entreaties, tears, will obtain no pity; when once the day of grace is shut: If Christ be not received, and the heart made obedient to his counsel in this world, the sinner is lost, and shall be rejected by the Lord forever. Oh that word "eternity!" How full of dread is it to them that live and die children of wrath! And yet how few are there that now lay these things to heart? And are seriously concerned to fly from the wrath which is to come! One would think the thoughts of Eternal Judgment, should make the boldest sinner tremble, and should turn the sweet morsels of his iniquity into gravel-stones, and make that which he now drinks down like water, to become as gall and wormwood to him. But alas! So wicked is the heart of man, and desperately bent on a sinful course; that unless he be renewed by effectual grace, no persuasion will prevail with him to forsake those ways, which lead to that place of torment where there is weeping and wailing, and gnashing of teeth for evermore.

FINIS.

SCRIPTURE INDEX

Old Testament

Genesis
1:1-2,26 55
2:1 32
4:1 32 n15
4:2 43

Exodus
15:18 207 n11
20:11 32

Deuteronomy
26:19 75
32:18 43 n17

Joshua
2:11 29

Ruth
1:8 193

1 Samuel
15:35 201
17:29 16

1 Kings
8:27 29

2 Kings
8:10 155

1 Chronicles
14:17 88
16:36 207 n10
29:10 207 n10

2 Chronicles
18:18 32

Job
14:4 126
15:7 43 n17
15:15 31
33:4 55
34:13 84
36:14 196
38:7 57
39:1 43 n17

Psalms
2:7 34
8:1 30
9:6 207 n11
10:16 207 n11
19 106

19:1-2 105
19:7-11 106
21:5 207 n11
22:18 187
22:27 84
24:1 84
29:9 43 n17, 44
33:6 32, 40, 198
41:14 207 n10
45:7,18 207 n11
45:14 73
48:4-5 32 n7
48:15 207 n11
51:5 43, 126
51:7 43 n17
52:10 207 n11
58:3 130
73:12 84
89:31 162
90:2 84
98:7 84
103:17 207 n10
104:5 207 n11
106:48 207 n10
113:4-6 30
118:10 88
119:44 207 n11

219

125:1-2 156
139 29
145:1-2,21 207 n11
145:8-9 105
147:19-20 110
148:4-5 32

Proverbs
1:24-31 189
1:28 77
8:22 41, 42
8:24 43
8:23 42
8:25 42, 43
8:29-30 42
8:32 42
20:9 187
24:12 180
29:18 110
30:4 45
30:6 49

Ecclesiastes
9:10 189
10:13 182
12 180

Song of Solomon (Canticles)
5:8-9 76
6:1 76
6:8-9 75
9:6 74

Isaiah
1:9 196
1:10 196
4:5 156
6 61
13:11 84
41:4 53
43:11 53
47:7 75
51:2 17 n17
53:6,11 170
54:8-10 156
55:3 133
55:6 189
57:13 31 n6
57:15 30, 31
66:8 43 n17

Jeremiah
7:7 207, 207 n10
10:25 110
23:24 29

25:5 207, 207 n10
27:7 88
31:3 156
31:34 91
32:39-40 156

Ezekiel
16:46,49 194
16:55,61 194
16:58 197
36:26-27 156
36:27 158

Daniel
12:3 207

Amos
8:9-14 110

Micah
4:5 207 n11
5:2 42

Zephaniah
2:9 195

New Testament

Matthew
3:12 183
3:17 42
5:25-26 200
7:13-15 79
7:14 202
7:15-16 2
7:21-23 77
8:22 85
10:22 147
10:41-42 77
11:19 41
12:24 187
12:31-32 186
12:31 185, 188
12:32 187, 188
12:36-37 180
13:40-41 77
17:5 42
18:7 84
18:15 196
18:34-35 200
20:16 77, 78, 78 n14
22:12 203
22:12-13 77
22:14 78
24 203
24:14 84
24:51 77
25 181, 204
25:1-12 76
25:32 180
25:41,46 203
26:13 84
28:19-20 102
28:20 208

Mark
3:28 185
3:29 208
9:43-44 183
10:31 78, 78 n14
16:15 102
20:31 78 n14

Luke
2:1 84, 87
2:13 32
11:42 90
12:10 185
12:47-48 200
12:58-59 200
12:59 201
13:24 202
16:8 84
16:23 212
17:10 180
18:11 90 n13
18:12 90
20:26 204

John
1 36, 45
1:1 43
1:2 42
1:2,14 46
1:10 86, 87
1:11 85
1:12 87, 171
1:23 42
1:29 92
3:5 111
3:5-7 129
3:6 86, 126
3:13-14 60
3:16 34, 67, 84
3:17 86
3:19 98, 99
3:36 95
4:5 84
4:42 84

6:27 145	**15:19** 84	**Romans**
6:33,51 84	**15:26** 35	**1:5** 88
6:37 69, 89	**16:1** 84	**1:8** 84
6:38 58	**16:11,33** 85	**1:19** 111
6:39-40 156	**16:28** 57	**1:19-20** 99, 106
6:40 67	**17:3** 109	**1:19-21** 108
6:42 59	**17:5** 57	**1:21** 128
6:44 118	**17:20** 111	**2:1** 108
6:45 118	**17:21** 84	**2:4** 105
6:51,58 208	**17:25** 84	**2:7** 67
7:4 84	**18:36** 84	**2:14** 79
7:7 84, 85		**2:14-16** 79
8:26 88	**Acts**	**2:15** 99
8:31 67	**2:17** 90	**2:16** 180
8:42,58 57	**3:15** 49	**3:6,19** 84
9:4 189	**3:19-20** 188	**3:20-22,28** 171
10:28-29 156	**3:21** 96	**3:21** 79
10:30 50	**4:12** 106	**3:22** 170
11:51-52 94	**4:27-28** 153	**3:24** 170
12:19 84, 88	**5:13** 75	**4:4-5** 170, 171
12:32 60, 89, 91	**10:12** 90	**4:7-8** 100
12:41 61	**10:34-35** 79	**4:13** 84
12:48 214	**13:48** 70	**5** 126, 127
14:6 109	**14:16** 110	**5:8,10** 94
14:17,22 84	**17:24** 84	**5:12** 84
14:30 85	**17:31** 180	**5:17** 171
15:4-6 157	**20:28** 38	**5:18** 91, 127
15:5 143	**20:30** 15	**5:19** 170

6 180
6:14 133
6:17 193
7 130
7:8 127
7:15-16 129
7:24 129
8:1 130
8:7 118
8:9 35
8:26 140
8:28 65
8:29 47
8:29-30 65, 156
8:32 170
8:38-39 156
9 132
9:5 49
9:16-22 164
9:22-23 152, 198
10:14 99, 107
10:18 84, 105, 106
11 132
11:6 65
11:7 70
11:12,15 84
12:2 84
13:14 127

14:2 90
14:10 180
16:25 208

1 Corinthians
1:5 90
1:20-21 84, 116
1:30 41
2:7-9 116
2:8 49
2:12 85
2:14 116
3:14-15 183
3:18-19 84
4:5 180
4:7 144
4:9 84
6:2 84
7:31,33 84
11:19 1
11:32 84
12:7 93
15:21 97
15:22 91, 96, 97
15:24 200
15:45-50 97

2 Corinthians
3:5 138
3:7 134
4:4 85
5:1 33
5:10 180
5:10-11 210
5:17 141
5:19 84, 92, 93
8:12 133

Galatians
1:4 84
2:15 170
2:16 171
3:10-11 111
3:11-12 170, 171
3:13 100, 170
4:1,4 84
4:4,6 58
4:6 60
4:25 134
5:3-4 133
5:19 127
6:14 84

Ephesians
1:4 47, 84

1:5 65
1:7 170
1:19-20 141
2:1 119
2:2 84, 208
2:3 95, 127, 129
2:8-10 170
2:10 141
2:12 110
2:21-22 31
4:4-5 75
4:10 60, 91
4:14 67
4:24 141
6:12 85

Philippians
1:6 163
2 36, 48
2:13 145

Colossians
1:6 84
1:15 42, 52
1:15-16 44
1:15-17 52
1:16 52
1:17 52

1:18 52
1:20 94
1:21 93, 94
1:21-23 147
1:21,23 67
1:23 102, 103, 104
2:8 84
2:11 127
2:15 42 n13

1 Thessalonians
5:23-24 156

2 Thessalonians
1:9 183
2:10-12 128

1 Timothy
1:9 47
1:19 159
1:19-20 162
2 214
2:1-3 91
2:4 90 n16
2:5 38
2:6 92
2:15 147
4:10 198

2 Timothy
1:9 42, 65
1:12 163
1:15 162
2:6 88
2:18-19 160
2:19 70
4:10 84

Titus
1:2 162, 208

Philemon
5:15 208

Hebrews
1:2 44, 55
1:3 35
1:8-9 56
2:5 188
2:9 92
2:16 56
3:6 148
4:1 162
4:2 134
5:9 67
6:2 213
6:4-6 147, 160, 186

6:5 188
8:11 91
9:11 84
9:15 173
11:6 107
11:38 84
12:9 67

James
1:14-15 129, 131
1:18 78, 111, 141
1:27 84
4:4 84
5:3 214

1 Peter
1:2 65, 67
1:3-5 156
1:11 61, 190
1:20 48
1:20-21 109
3:19 212
3:19-20 190
4:5 180
4:6 190

2 Peter
1:4 141

2:5 84, 190
2:20 147
3:9 197
3:17 1

1 John
2:2 84, 92, 93
2:15-17 84
2:19 148, 156, 166
3:16 38
4:5 84
5:7 34
5:19 84, 95

Jude
7 196

Revelation
2:12,15 70
3:5 70, 71
5:9 89
7:8 196
13:3 84
14:10 198
14:11 207, 183
14:14 78
18:3,23 88
18:7 75

19:3 207
20:10 207
20:12 180
20:12,15 71
20:15 186
21:7 73
21:8 76, 186, 187
22:14 67
22:14-15 76
22:16 61
22:19 70, 71